I have never in my life

I have never in my life

Don Jenrette

Deeds Publishing | Athens

Published by Deeds Publishing in Athens, GA
www.deedspublishing.com

Printed in The United States of America

Cover design by Mark Babcock. Text layout by Matt King

ISBN 978-1-947309-50-0

Books are available in quantity for promotional or premium use. For information, email info@deedspublishing.com.

First Edition, 2018

10 9 8 7 6 5 4 3 2 1

For my wife Faye, my children Jennifer, Roxanne, and Edwin, to my grandchildren Tre', Jacob, Madison, Sophie, and Tucker, to my other kinfolk, my friends, my Christian friends, and to those past, present, and future who choose to wear the uniform of the United States Armed Forces.

The reason why I entitled my book "I Have Never in My Life", my daughter-in-law Ashley suggested it because we cannot count the number of times my wife has said those words after I've said or done something she didn't deeply appreciate.

Contents

Long-sleeved Flannel Shirt

MANY YEAR AGO, WHILE ATTENDING A FESTIVAL OF SORTS in downtown Macon, I had eaten something that was not agreeing with me. It was night time, chilly, damp, and the lines to the Port-A-Potties seemed a mile long each — all 10-15 of them. So, I trotted to the back of line in one of them, hoping and praying that I'd make it in time. Finally, after what seemed to be an eternity, I arrived inside one of them. As I proceeded to do my business, I noticed that all the toilet paper had been thrown into the hole in the potty. I initially hesitated to continue on but it was too late. Soon thereafter I started to worry about what to do without any toilet paper. So, I bowed my head and began to pray.

After praying, I looked up and to my amazement there appeared a long-sleeved flannel shirt, over in the corner — I didn't see when I first got in there. So, I picked up the shirt, turned one sleeve inside out and used it, paying very close attention to the location of the button on it. After using it, my first inclination was to throw it into the hole, but decided that the owner might come back for it, or I, or someone else, might need another answered prayer later that night. Seeing a flannel shirt now takes on a new meaning for me.

Saint Augustine

The only time I ever played hooky from school—I got caught. I was in the 10th grade, waiting at the bus stop for my morning ride to Cook High School. Before boarding the bus, three of my buddies came up in an old hoopty-ride the size of a medium sized boat. The owner of the ride, Wayne, asked me if I was interested in going with them to Saint Augustine, Florida. Being young and foolish, I said yes. It was a Friday but I had no idea at the time that the trip to Florida was going to turn into a two-night stay—bear in mind, also without asking or getting my Ma's approval for my going on the misguided trip.

On our way out of town, we passed our school principal on his way into work and knew that we had just been had. Several miles down the road, I learned the real reason I was asked to come along. You see, Wayne, along with my other two friends, Johnny and Dale, didn't have enough lunch room money on them to pay for the gasoline to fill up the hoopty-ride's gas tank. So, I gave up my last 30 cents. After that, I asked the all-important question, "Why are we going to Saint Augustine?" To which my friends replied, "To look for women". After pondering the answer to my question, I asked my second question, "What do we do when we find some?"

By the time we arrived in Saint Augustine, we all four were hungry—with not even two nickels to rub together. But we toughed it out and with no money for lodging, we slept in the hoopty-ride for two nights. Wayne slept in the front seat, Johnny in the back seat, Dale was small enough to perch against the back window, and I slept in the floorboard of the backseat. After getting a belly full of Saint Augustine, we headed back home for more familiar surroundings, a good meal, and some good rest.

I was dropped off first that Sunday morning, very close to the lunch time hour. Upon arriving at my Ma Smith's home, I saw that my Uncle Bill's Pontiac convertible was there. Oh no! My Uncle Bill was my mama's sole surviving brother and was a man's man—big, burly—and had been a bouncer at numerous juke joints in neighboring Valdosta and a lawman for the City of Hahira and for the Lowndes County Georgia Sheriff's Department. He also wore a thick policeman's belt around his waist and always kept a spare at Ma's house.

Well, when I walked into the house, I smelled fried pork chops—and to a teenager's very empty stomach, it was heaven on earth. Next, Uncle Bill asked me where I had been since Friday, to which I told him the true story of going with my friends to Saint Augustine—but I left out the part about "to look for women." Fearing that Uncle Bill was about to take his police belt out and tan my backside, he asked me if I was hungry. To which I replied a resounding yes. So we sat down, me, Ma, Uncle Bill, and my two sisters, Susan and Jane. Here's what the lunch consisted of: fried pork chops, creamed potatoes with brown gravy, kernel corn, green beans, cake and sweet iced tea. And I inhaled it.

After finishing my lunch, I began to ease toward the direction of my bedroom in the back of Ma's Jim Walter built home. Just before I got to my bedroom door, Uncle Bill asked me what I was doing. I told him politely that I was going to rest since I had not slept good for two nights. Uncle Bill's reply was, "Not now, son." Fearing that the whipping of all whippings was about to commence, he told me to sit in the chair next to the heater. Bear in mind that we only had one chair in our whole house that did not have arms on it—yes, it was that one. So, I sat in it, and sat in it, and fell out of it twice. Finally, at 8:30 that night, Uncle Bill told me I could get my bath and go to bed, and to be in school on the next day.

You see, Mr. Whitfield, high school principal, had called my Ma and told her he had seen me and Wayne, Johnny, and Dale heading out of town when we should have been in school. This was my one and only time playing hooky from school. Oh, we never found any women.

Twins in the E.R.

SEVERAL YEARS AGO, MY MOTHER-IN-LAW TOOK SICK ON A weekend and we took her to the local Emergency Room (E.R.) She was eventually placed into one of the triage rooms for further medical evaluation. By the way, each of those rooms has only one door that serves as an entrance and exit point. The nurse that was attending to my mother-in-law apparently was also attending to the patient in the adjoining triage room. As fate would have it, my friend Harold's sister-in-law was in the next room to my mother-in-law's room that day. Harold is a big ole boy like me. As a matter of fact, one of the women in our church mistook Harold for me one Sunday and hugged him, telling him she enjoyed the previous sermon I preached.

Well, the nurse, after leaving my mother-in-law's bedside with me and my wife Faye inside, went to the room next door—Harold's sister-in-law's room. Within 10-15 minutes, the nurse came in to check on my mother-in-law and looked at me and said, "Now how did you get here before me?" My wife wanted to know what I did this time. I didn't know what the nurse meant until I saw her go to the room next door and learned later she asked my friend Harold the same question. Dumbfounded, he didn't know what she meant either.

However, it all came together a little while later when the nurse saw both Harold and me standing side by side in the hallway between the two triage rooms. Hence, twins in the E.R.

Jimmy's Right Pinky

DURING THE MID TO LATE 1980s, I SERVED AS A SQUADRON Commander at Chanute AFB's Technical Training base in East Central Illinois. It's now closed down. I had the responsibility for the lodging, morale and welfare, and technical training for over 1,000 AF trainees, it was an awesome opportunity for me. Additionally, I had a staff of one first lieutenant, a first sergeant, and numerous non-commissioned officers, and a couple of administrative clerks who were young airmen. I served in that role for over two year but have one specific story I choose to share here.

His first name was Jimmy (not his real name, but we'll use it). His home was Louisiana. His responsibility for a twelve month stretch of time was to maintain his military bearing and to successfully learn and graduate technical school to serve as an aircraft mechanic at another active duty AF base. There was one catch for Jimmy—his wife, initially unbeknownst to us, forwarded a snail mail to me as his commanding officer. It was in the days before emails, tweets, and the sort. The letter told me and the Staff Judge Advocate's

(SJA) Office that she was legally married to Jimmy and she needed a military dependent's identification card in order for her to receive medical treatments and commissary and Base Exchange privileges.

My Orderly Room checked Jimmy's locator card he accomplished upon his arrival at Chanute from boot camp. He circled his marital status as Single and not Married. I asked my first sergeant to call him on the carpet and provide an explanation to me. Jimmy told us he married the woman in question when he was 16 and she was 14, in Mexico, and did not believe it was a legal marriage. After consultation with my SJA, he asked that the "wife" provide written support of their lawful marriage in Mexico.

Months passed by and we received a copy of the marriage certificate—in Spanish. After review by the SJA, we sent it to the closest Mexican Consulate's Office asking for their reading and legal review. Months ensued, but before learning that the marriage was indeed a legal one, Jimmy's wife sent another letter alleging that she had further proof of her husband and his previous stint as a Satanist Priest back in the home state of Louisiana. She further stated that her husband's right pinky finger had been severed as a part of the Satanist Priest ritual years before.

Curious about it, we called Jimmy into my office and when he saluted my uniform upon entry, we could tell he was missing his right pinky finger. Weeks later, we received notification that their marriage was legal and I gave Jimmy a direct order to get the proper paperwork to his wife so she could obtain and use a military dependent's identification card.

Fortunately for Jimmy, before his time was up at Chanute, I was sent for a three-month professional military education opportunity and left my lieutenant in charge. I told my lieutenant to accomplish the discharge paperwork for Jimmy and send him back to Louisiana if he slipped up one more time. When I returned back to Chanute, I asked about the status of Jimmy and learned that he had successfully graduated and was sent to an active duty base to serve as an aircraft mechanic.

As fate would have it, almost two years later I was traveling on a military aircraft and stopped to refuel at a base in Japan and ran up on none other than Jimmy—standing there with his uniform blouse on and it was very noticeable that he had lost the only two stripes he had. I asked him why and he said he had gotten a Japanese lady pregnant and was not showing up at work on time and his excuses continued to grow. I asked him about his wife and family in Louisiana and he said they had divorced earlier that year.

I told him he needed to get his life straight once the AF sent him back home to stay. And yes, I noticed he was still missing his right pinky finger.

Singing in the Church

In the late 1990s, I was asked by my niece Tracy if I would perform a solo at her home church in Blue Ridge, Georgia. Excited that she thought I was good enough to sing in her church, I accepted. Come to think of it, the only times Tracy ever heard me singing was during Karoke contests at Christmas.

The time came and upon my arrival at the church the pastor met me and asked what I planned to sing. I told him. Unknowingly, the choir sang that same song prior to my stab at it. While they were singing, the pastor came to my seat and, knowing that I planned to sing that same song, he told me it would be okay to sing it again solo. However, I then thumbed through the Baptist Hymnal and decided to sing *How Great Thou Art*, accompanied by the church pianist.

Unfortunately, I failed to practice with her before the performance—a decision I immediately regretted once she started me off in a key much too high. But I pressed on, and then to make matters worse, she stopped playing the piano, so I wound up singing the remainder of the song alone. While

I was singing, I began to pop a sweat to beat all sweats. And, looking for moral support from my family members, I could see that none of them were looking at me and instead had their heads down — either praying or shame-faced, or both.

Once I was through, I walked back to sit with my wife and family to which my wife told me to go to the rest room and wipe my face off. Being a good husband, I did so. However, the bathroom lacked two things — paper towels and a mirror. Not being out done, I washed my face and used toilet tissue to wipe my face off. Unknowingly, I had left some of the toilet paper on my face. When I sat down with my family, they said I looked like I had cut my face shaving and tried to stop the bleeding with the toilet paper.

Needless to say, that was going to be my first and only time singing a solo in any church house. My niece who asked me to sing that day told me that that church was struck by lightning and burned to the ground later. Oh, and I've never been asked to sing at any church by any of my family members since.

Singing in the Church II

Taking the vow that I would never sing aloud by myself in church again, I did seize the opportunity to lead a congregation of church members in a church in Byron, Georgia. Allow me to set the scene. After my son-in-law, Ryan, was killed riding his motorcycle when a deer knocked him off it, I felt God's Call on my life to serve Him as a Minister of the Gospel.

In November 2013, I was licensed to preach and was asked by a small church in Byron to preach the Gospel Message since they were looking for a full time preacher. The congregation had around 30 people at the time. I wound up preaching there around 6-8 times. Unfortunately, during one of those morning worship hours the song leader was not present so the Chairman of Deacons asked me to lead the singing prior to the service. Even after I shared with him what had happened at the church in Blue Ridge, he told me everything would be fine.

Well, as God is my witness, once I started leading the congregation in singing from the Baptist Hymnal, from the distance came the sound of car alarms from the church parking lot. And you should have seen the look on the Chairman of the Deacons' face! Again, I made the vow never to sing or to lead the singing in any church. The Bible tells us about the spiritual gifts God has given us. Mine is preaching and not singing.

The Binion Building

AFTER COMPLETING 24 YEARS OF MILITARY SERVICE IN THE United States Air Force, my family and I moved back to Georgia. I worked in the Prison Ministry as a Counselor at one of two women's prisons in the state. As a part of my on-going training, I, along with a dozen or so prison employees, went to the State Mental Hospital which was then in Milledgeville. The training lasted for two days with one night lodging there. In an effort to save state tax payer's money we stayed in one of the vacant hospital buildings. I was told the morning after the night of lodging that I kept up most of my colleagues because of my snoring. Unknowingly, it was their chance to get back at me for their bad night's sleep.

The second day, we toured the Binion Building. The building at that time was set aside to house those deemed criminally insane. Our tour guides were prison guards and administrators. We first were led into a room where two guards were charged with watching over an inmate that reminded me of Dr. Hannibal Lecter—yeah, you know the one in the movie *Silence of the Lambs*. From there we went into a dayroom where the inmates were "watching" TV. And finally we were led into an outside fenced-in basketball court area. Once we entered into the Binion Building, we were each issued a personal ID card with a lanyard to hang around our necks to readily distinguish us from the inmates. Well, as fate would have it, I became so enthralled in looking at the inmates inside that fence that to my shock when I looked around for the rest of my colleagues, no one was there—no one but the prison guards and the inmates—and me.

Startled, I approached one of the guards and upon showing him my ID card around my neck and telling him I had been left behind, he replied to me that, "anyone can get one of those." To which I began to feel the sweat dripping down my back for fear that I was being mistaken for a criminally insane inmate in the Binion Building. Finally, in what seemed to be an eternity, one of the other guards came to me and told me it was a prank hatched by my prison colleagues.

After that I made sure I was not left alone in the Binion Building and never lodged again with my prison colleagues.

Carl

IN MY YOUNGER DAYS, I ENJOYED PLAYING RACQUETBALL during my lunch breaks. And I would play with anyone. One day an older gentleman asked me to play with him and I did. His name was Carl. Every day for weeks, Carl and I met to play racquetball at Robins AFB in 1975. Actually, we shared equal racquetball skills, which made it enjoyable and challenging.

One day after receiving notification from my colonel that I had been selected by the AF Manpower Personnel Center to ship out for Utapao, Thailand with only three months remaining at Robins, my racquetball game was apparently suffering. To make matters worse, I had met the woman I had planned to make my wife and just knew that if I left for Thailand she could find another to wed instead of me. Carl noticed that I was not playing to my potential and asked me what was wrong that fateful day. I told him and he told me not to worry about it. That was easy for him to say since he was not in my shoes. We continued to play during that lunch hour.

The next morning upon arriving at my desk, my colonel called me in and, to my astonishment, informed me that my orders for Thailand were cancelled. I was elated! During my lunch hour racquetball match with Carl, he noticed that I again had that spring in my step that he had grown accustomed to and asked me why. I told him my orders to Thailand had been cancelled. He then unraveled the mystery of how they were cancelled. He told me that after our conversation the day before, he personally contacted the two-star general in charge of the AF Manpower Personnel Center in San Antonio and told him he did not want to lose his racquetball partner, Don Jenrette.

Astonished—I asked him how he had that kind of power. He then told me he had flown F-86s in Korea with that general officer and he owed him a favor. I then asked him what his job was there at Robins. He told me he was the Vice Commander of the Center and that he was a one-star general. Carl later earned his second star and was transferred to Tinker AFB in Oklahoma where he was their Center commander before his retirement. Thank God for His perfect timing and my chance encounters playing racquetball with an older gentleman named Carl.

Guam Intervention

From 1978 to 1980, I served on the island of Guam at Andersen AFB as a drug/alcohol counselor. A part of my job was to view the daily cop blotter every morning to ascertain if anyone had been arrested for a drug or alcohol related incident overnight. One morning after reading that a young two-striper had been found face down in the ditch between the club and the dormitories, I contacted his first sergeant about it. The Munitions Maintenance Squadron where he worked had nearly 1,000 Airmen assigned and, as I recall, the airman in question had a very common name.

Within 30 minutes, the airman with that name arrived in my office for a personal intervention regarding the previous night's event. Unexpectedly, the airman showed up looking extremely sharp — bright-eyed and bushy-tailed. A part of my training was the keen awareness of the abuser and his or her over compensation to not looking or acting the part of substance abuser. I felt this was the case with this airman and proceeded for the next hour and a half to break his insistence that he had not been found in the ditch that previous night drunk as Cooter Brown. I don't think I've ever met the original Cooter Brown but I've been around plenty of his look alikes.

After I released the young airman, I telephoned his first sergeant and explained the airman's denial. At that the first sergeant checked his muster rolls and found the same name, and it belonged to another man. At that he sent him to me for questioning. At first glance, I knew at last I had the right airman. After that I always checked the counselee's name and serial number.

And, in 1982, after being selected to train every new AF drug and alcohol counselor, I shared that same story with them to save them the unnecessary time and embarrassment — for the airmen in question and for the counselor.

341s

From 1983 to 1986, I served numerous roles as a newly minted second lieutenant. Frankly, my wish is that everyone in the military should experience what it's like to be a second lieutenant. When I pinned on my second lieutenant bars, I had already served as a non-commissioned officer for the previous 12 years, rising to the rank of Technical Sergeant (E-6).

The location of my tenure as a second lieutenant was at Keesler AFB, Biloxi, Mississippi — a military technical school environment. The objective of such a location is to ensure the airmen continued in their transition from being a civilian to being a military member, and to learn their military technical skills through rigorous in-classroom instruction. The Air and Education Training Command, in its efforts to instill military discipline, developed and implemented an AF Form called the 341. Two 341s, by AF instruction, were to be on the person of every trainee in case a superior — even a newly minted second lieutenant — saw an infraction and pointed it out to the perpetrator by "pulling" the 341 from the airmen. If a 341 was pulled, it could adversely affect the privilege of named airmen in receiving base liberty or even a bus trip to the local shopping mall or movie theatre. It has been said of the 341, an airman had rather have his arm chopped off than to get a 341 "pulled".

As fate would have it, I was walking from my office building down four blocks to our headquarters building — wearing my AF uniform and my flight cap. For you who do not know about the flight cap, for the officers it has on it what some refer to as Christmas tinsel and the rank of the officer is pinned on the front right side of the cap. While walking to my headquarters building, numerous airmen failed to salute the uniform I was wearing — so I began "pulling" 341s from each. Some of them even told me they had never had one "pulled" and were devastated as I continually stuffed my pants pockets with them. While approaching the headquarters building, which had a large glass enclosure on the outside, I noticed my profile as I passed. To my amazement, I then saw the reason why the airmen failed to salute my uniform. Background information, an unwritten rule for any military member who approaches a fellow member outside is to look carefully at their "cover" or cap or hat even before looking at the uniform.

I had placed my flight cap on backward, with my second lieutenant rank facing the back. Doing the right thing, I immediately tore up all the 341s and told no one about what had happened — for years and years. As an NCO I had never, ever, done that, but as a second lieutenant I had temporarily lost my mind.

Halloween in Mississippi

WHILE STATIONED IN MISSISSIPPI FROM 1983 TO 1986, OUR children were in their formative years of development. My wife, Faye, chose not to work outside the home and to instead raise our children. It was a decision we both knew was best for our family. Well, my wife tried the Officers Wives Club meetings, but it was not her cup of tea (pun intended). So, she started babysitting others' children. At one time, she had 23 children she took care of daily—counting our own three. She fed them, bedded them down, played with them, etc. The mothers of these children grew to love Faye, so much so that even when they didn't have anything else to do, they would take their child or children to stay with Faye. I thank God that my wife is given the gift of working and loving children. Not everyone is. I'm one of them that does not have that gift.

So, it was seldom that I got to see many of the children except toward the end of each military day when their parents came to pick them up. One Halloween, Faye took our children trick or treating and I had the task of handing out the candy at our home—on the front porch. While performing that role, I remember a family approaching with their children in tow that Faye had babysat regularly. I heard one of the mothers ask her child if she knew who I was and the toddler replied, "That's Mr. Faye."

When King Got Shot

My final job in the Department of Defense was working as the Air Force Reserve's Drug Demand Reduction Program Manager. In essence, that meant I was responsible for random drug testing and prevention education efforts for 66 hospitals in 29 states for the AF Reserve. That job required many temporary duty assignments, commonly referred to as TDYs. One of those TDYs took me to the west coast of the U.S. After performing the mission out there, I was boarding a commercial airliner and wound up sitting with a young lady returning home to Florida from vacation. Our seats were in the forward area of the coach class where we could see the first-class passengers come on board for their nice, more comfortable seats.

One of the passengers was Andrew Young. Making chit chat before we pushed back from the gate area I asked the young lady if she recognized who that man was. She told me no. At that I began telling her that he was the former U.S. Congressman from Georgia, the former United Nations Ambassador under President Jimmy Carter, and that the man was with King when he got shot. To my surprise, she replied by saying, "I remember when Rodney King got shot."

That story should remind us all of the generation gap.

July 20, 1969

THAT'S THE DATE THAT MAN FIRST LANDED AND WALKED on the surface of the moon—so they say. My Ma Smith never believed that they actually walked on the moon that night, and instead they were probably in some warehouse out west somewhere filming it and making us believe so. She did believe in wrestling though. A lot of the old folks felt that way back then.

That same night, a Sunday, my friend and I had a double date with some girls. After the date, I went back home to my Ma's Jim Walter built house. Since it was approaching 11 o'clock, well past her bedtime, she was not interested in watching the television so I asked if I could go next door to my friend's house and watch it there. She agreed. So, we watched it with my friend's daddy and his two sons, similar to my age.

Their daddy had been drinking all that weekend and was three sheets in the wind. After we saw Neil Armstrong make his first step on the moon, my friend's daddy motioned all of us boys to come outside. Well, since we were raised to obey our elders, we did so. My friend's daddy apparently felt the same way my Ma did and that it was all a big hoax. At that he pointed up at the moon and gave us his proof that it was all fake news. My friend's daddy told us, looking at a quarter moon, that they were not on the moon because it wasn't even all up there that night. It reminds me that, no matter what, you can't convince everybody of everything.

Meeting the One and Only Guitar Man

THE GUITAR MAN WAS RECENTLY INDUCTED INTO THE Country Music Hall of Fame. Jerry Reed finally got his due. Unfortunately, he died many years ago and did not live to see this prestigious award bestowed upon him. But his girls were there, both of them. They shared Jerry's wit and humor — they said they were referred to as Daughter #1 and Daughter #2. Yep, he's the same one that was the truck driver in the Smokey and the Bandit movies and was handpicked by Elvis Presley to play the guitar licks in the song *Guitar Man*.

I got the opportunity to meet Jerry Reed back in 1988 while I was stationed in the Republic of South Korea. At the time, my job was serving as the Base Commander's executive officer — or better known as flunky or gopher — you know the type, go for this and go for that. When Jerry Reed and his band showed up, they first had a meeting with my colonel and, unbeknownst to me, he had told Jerry that I, too, was from the great state of Georgia. Jerry Reed called home the Atlanta, Georgia area.

As was customary, the night before any well-known band came to play for our troops in South Korea, we would feed them lunch. When my colonel introduced me to Jerry, I was introduced as Billy Bob from Georgia. Apparently, Jerry wanted to find out if I was really from Georgia and after I told him, "Mr. Reed, it's a pleasure to meet you." He replied, "My daddy went by Mr. Reed, please call me Jerry." He went further to see if I was really from the great state of Georgia. He asked me if I knew where Ty Ty was. I immediately told him it is west of Tifton on U.S. Highway 82. At that he gave me the seal of approval through a wink at my colonel and appointed me with the name Billy Bob also. Again, congratulations Jerry, for a long overdue recognition.

The Wrestling Move in the Double Wide

DECADES AGO, WHEN MY MA SMITH DIED, WE ALL MET AS a family at the central location of one of my mama's surviving sisters, my Aunt Earline. Being one of the oldest cousins on my mama's side of the family, I had seized the opportunity to name our aunts and uncles before any of my younger siblings and cousins came along. Aunt Earline was Aunt Een. Why? Because as a young lad learning to speak, Aunt Earline was a mouthful to say, so I shortened it to Aunt Een. Her first husband's name was W.M. as is the custom for many a southern man to go by two letters of the alphabet. Again, apparently W.M. was too much of a mouthful to say so I called him Uncle Dub.

One of my cousins came from the Ocala, Florida area to attend Ma's funeral along with her husband named Angel. Angel was originally from Cuba and had hands the size of a catcher's mitt. Aunt Een's two boys got all liquored up that Saturday afternoon and while watching Florida Wrestling on the TV set they talked Angel into being a part of a wrestling move that had just seen performed. It was called the Sky-Lift Slam. It involved two wrestlers on each side of a third wrestler, holding each arm of the single wrestler, picking him up in the sky and slamming him in a backwards motion to the floor.

Apparently my three sheets in the wind cousins didn't know that the real wrestling rings had floors or mats that would give when impacted by human beings. My two cousins and Angel quickly learned that the floor in a double wide is not meant to be used to conduct a wrestling move like the Sky Lift Slam. I would not have believed this story when it was told to me unless I had actually seen the scene in person. Their wrestling move developed a hole in the floor that required the draping of a heavy tarp on it, anchored down by a cement block at the four corners. Also, you could see the black boot marks left by Angel's shoes at the top of the double wide. That was the Spring of 1989. We haven't seen Angel since.

You Can't Tell the Book by Looking at the Cover

DURING ONE OF THE FIRST TRIPS TO A DISNEY WORLD amusement park, I learned a valuable lesson in life. You can't tell the book by looking at the cover. Anyone who is familiar with visits to any of the Disney properties in the Orlando, Florida area knows that it's famous for the very long waiting times standing in line, sometimes up to an hour or more — for a 3-5 minute ride. Well, my wife and I were in such a line when I became bored and introduced myself and my wife to a nicely dressed family of four — a husband and his wife and two pre-teens. To me they looked Asian. After my introduction, the husband and wife simply gave us a non-verbal. Curious, I then asked the man, "Are y'all from, Japan? How long are y'all spending here?"

At that, the man replied to me in very good English, "Sir, the four of us were born and raised here in America." At that I turned around facing the crowd of people before me, embarrassed, and said the following to my wife, "Is this line moving any?" Sometimes you can't tell the book by looking at the cover.

Honeymoon Night in the Rocket Hotel

IMMEDIATELY AFTER LEAVING OUR WEDDING RECEPTION IN Hawkinsville, Georgia, my new bride and I lit out for Disney World in Florida. We had borrowed her Uncle D's pickup truck with the camper hull perched on the back of it. We did this for the sole purpose of saving money on expensive hotel rooms down in Orlando. Both of us were extremely tired and only got as far as 30 miles down the road, stopping in Cordele, the Watermelon Capital of the World. We had not made any reservations and were very fortunate to get a hotel room at what we now refer as the Rocket Hotel.

It wasn't officially named that, but for decades there has stood a landmark of sorts right off Interstate 75 at one of the three Cordele exits. It's an old Titan missile obtained from NASA many decades ago — high into the air and easy to see upon approach on I-75 both north and south bound. Well, as fate would have it, the only room left for us on that mid-June night in 1976 was located directly over the swimming pool area.

As my bride and I were ascending the stairs to our top

floor Honeymoon Suite (bear in mind it really wasn't) those splashing in that pool all stopped and noticed me when I performed the customary lifting and taking my bride across the threshold of our hotel room. We didn't really notice the attention we had garnered until we heard a loud applause and laughter from the folks gathered around that pool. After I got my bride settled in, I went back out to bring our luggage up to our room. Again, those around the pool stopped to watch me bring up the two pieces of luggage. However, once I got to the door of our hotel room I realized I had forgotten something very important — the hotel room keys.

Not being outdone and feeling the eyes of those gathered around the pool on me, I proceeded to knock on my hotel room to gain access by my bride. However, she didn't readily answer. So, I knocked again. No answer. The third time I knocked harder since maybe she just couldn't hear the knocking. At what seemed to be an eternity but was probably 10-15 minutes, I waited until she answered the door. And, I could hear the laughter of those same folks gathered around the pool, and probably thinking, "The boy's been locked out of his own hotel room on their wedding night!" The story's not over.

After finally gaining entrance, I learned that my bride had taken a shower and that was why she could not hear my knocking. Well, later that evening ... my bride and I heard a knock on our hotel room door and at that I jumped up, put on my clothes, and asked who was there. Back then I always slept in my birthday suit. No reply. So I opened the door and no one was in sight. I know it wasn't room service because the Rocket Hotel was not that kind of hotel.

Crawling back in to bed, I told my bride I didn't see anyone and it was, no doubt, someone that had been around the pool playing a prank on us. About five minutes later, another knock came on the door. At that I jumped up sooner in hopes I would catch the prankster(s). No luck. I then told my bride I was going to stay up and stand by the door so when they knocked the third time I would catch the person or persons.

I stood by the door. And I stood by the door a longer time. What lasted probably 10-15 minutes but seemed like a life time, no more knocks on our hotel room door. Disgusted that I had misjudged the prankster's timing, I voiced my disgust with my bride. But she didn't hear me — during those precious 10-15 minutes she had gone to sleep. That was the first and last overnight stay at the Rocket Hotel in Cordele, they tore it down to build a newer hotel.

Church Choirs to the Left of Me, Church Choirs to the Right

DURING A 14-MONTH PERIOD, MY WIFE UNDERWENT FOUR surgeries — one for her back, one for her knee, one for her hip, and one for her right shoulder. Along with that came a lot of doctor prescribed pain relieving medicines — none of which were prescribed for me. In preparation for a Temporary Duty trip for my civil service job at Robins AFB, I ensured I had packed all my necessary clothes, toiletries, and personal medicines. However, atypical of my preparations, I laid my daily medications near where my wife had placed her daily meds, to include those pain pills. As is the custom, I take my daily meds with my protein milk. After shaking my milk as the instructions suggest, I mistakenly picked up my wife's meds, placed them all in my mouth, and swallowed them down with a huge gulp of my protein milk. And, as soon as I swallowed them I looked down at the counter and saw my own meds sitting there and not my wife's. Knowing that my commercial airliner was due to leave the Atlanta Airport within the next three hours, I began to scurry around to get my bags in my truck for the trip—to make it there on time.

Before my wife left our home for Sunday School, I told her what I had done and I asked her what her physical and mental reaction was to any and all of those medications. She told me it helped ease her pain during some very painful times of recovery. Then I asked her two other important questions for me—why I asked those I still don't know, but the pills might have already begun to kick into my system. The first question was, "Are you still on The Pill?" And the last question was, "Are your meds time released or do they hit you all at once?"

Her answer to the first question was an emphatic no, and her second answer was that they hit her all at once. After she left for church, I proceeded to drag my one piece of luggage to my truck in what is about 20-30 yards from my garage door to where I park my truck. It seemed like it was two football fields away from me. And to make matters worse, while placing my luggage into my back seat, I began to hear a beautiful sound—a church choir sound coming from an area just south of my parking location among some pine trees. Deep down I knew something wasn't right.

Then, the church choir switched places on me. The sound then came from the road in front of our home. It was highly unusual! So, I staggered back to the house, got the rest of my traveling papers, and jumped into the driver's seat of my pickup truck, heading from Bonaire to the Atlanta Airport—a 110 mile trip, mostly on Interstate 75 North to the outskirts of Georgia's capital city. Oh, and my work colleague who lived in Perry, Georgia, just south of me had already left for the airport and I chose not to ask him to turnaround to pick me up because of my self-induced predicament.

The only thing I remember about the trip up I-75 is it didn't seem to take as long as it usually did. At one point during the trip I started to see wavy, squiggly shapes in front of me and pulled off at the High Falls exit, almost 60 miles from my home. My thought process was that maybe some fresh air away from my steering wheel would clear my head. But it didn't. After I literally fell out of my truck, holding on dearly to the sides, I realized I couldn't even stand up, much less drive myself safely to the Airport—another 50 plus miles away. So, I crawled back in my truck, said a prayer, sat there for a while, and then drove back onto the interstate.

Fortunately, and thankful to God I made it to the airport self-parking lot, I boarded the bus to the terminal and, as fate would have it, my coworker was waiting with his luggage checking in at the ticket counter. And immediately he could tell something was wrong, even before I told him about my misfortune. He physically assisted me through the TSA area and to our airport gate where we would board the plane taking us to the Pittsburgh airport. By the time we got to Pittsburgh, I was much better, but had to change the name of the driver of our rental car from my name to his.

Thinking back on it, both choirs sang beautifully that morning, the one to the left of me, and the one to the right.

Scratching Off Our Bucket List

SEVERAL YEARS BACK, THERE WAS A MOVIE ENTITLED *BUCK-et List* with Morgan Freeman and Robert DeNiro. They were two friends set to visit specific areas of the globe before they "kicked the bucket". It got my wife and me to thinking that same thing. We started our own bucket list. Since that time, we have been fortunate enough to begin scratching off specific locations, too. Here goes.

The first trip was Niagara Falls. We even got our passports updated to visit the falls on the Canadian side. We took our then 6-year-old granddaughter, Madison. We were not disappointed—it was beautiful, specifically during the night time with all the colored lights on it. Also, we did the Maid of the Mist trip where we experienced riding through the waves of the Niagara River and felt the mist of the falls. A lifetime experience indeed.

Another trip was to see the Green Mountains of Vermont. My wife went with me on a TDY trip to attend a training conference in Burlington, Vermont. Fortunately, it was during the summer time and Madison went along with us. While I was at work that week, my wife and granddaughter visited the Ben and Jerry's Ice Cream factory located not far from Burlington. They brought me back a tee shirt that I still have. We also got to take a ferry across Lake Champlain. The most striking thing to us about Vermont was the beauty of the Green Mountains and the ride through the small hamlets in that state. In most of the little towns they had statues of cows painted with multi-colors. We assumed because Ben and Jerry's is famous for using their Vermont cows for the cream in their ice cream flavors. All in all, it was a nice visit.

The next "bucket list" trip was to the Big Apple. Yep, my wife, our daughter Roxanne and granddaughter Madison went up there for the Macy's Thanksgiving Day Parade. For decades, my wife dreamed of seeing it live since she only got to see the taped version after cooking every Thanksgiving meal for the family for decades.

I went through a travel agency there and scheduled our arrival by commercial airline to the Newark, New Jersey airport on the Tuesday prior to Thanksgiving. My daughter Roxanne had not traveled on a commercial airliner for years and got a dose of the TSA procedures at the Atlanta Airport. They confiscated her large bottles of hair shampoo and conditioner, soap, and the like. She told us later that she was so frustrated at that process that she was ready to head back home.

Once we arrived at New York City, we purchased the same items in smaller containers that TSA accepts for boarding. While riding in an airport van designed to take us from the airport to our downtown hotel near Time Square, we could tell we were in the Big Apple. Madison told us in preparation for the visit that she wanted to experience the following: a ride in a New York City taxi, a ride on the subway, a visit to the Statue of Liberty, and to see the Broadway production of *The Lion King*. And we all experienced them. However, the most fun of the whole trip was riding in one of those bicycle powered rickshaws from the Broadway play back to our hotel—a three-block experience. We took two of them, one for Madison and me, and one for my wife and Roxanne. What an experience! That was Tuesday night.

On Wednesday, we took a scheduled tour of Wall Street, the church and its property who actually own all the property down there, and saw the spot where Queen Elizabeth II stood in the front of that church decades ago. Also, we went to the location where the Macy's crew blow up each of the balloons that would fly over during the long trek through the Big Apple on Thanksgiving Day. The floats were huge.

Then came Thanksgiving Day. We had breakfast on the run and arrived by New York City taxi to the corner of 72nd Street and Central Park—30 blocks from our hotel near Times Square. We found out later that the parade went directly beside the hotel we stayed in, but Madison got her taxi ride in the Big Apple. We got to our designated locale around 6:45 a.m. with the parade beginning at 9 a.m. Already the crowd was three rows deep and by the time the parade started, it was 20-30 rows deep with observers like us.

What struck me most about that morning was the temperature was uncommonly warm for that time of year up there, it got up into the 60s that day. And the security was massive. Huge police vehicles dotted the street landscapes everywhere and a police helicopter hovered over the sky line. After the parade, we took another taxi back to our hotel and enjoyed a catered Thanksgiving dinner across the street from our hotel. We sat with a couple from Boston, Massachusetts, and others from Colorado. It was a fine meal. We ate turkey, dressing, and all the fixings, plus tables of food with sweets. And we got some sweet iced tea — well, it was unsweetened but we added some pink packet sweetener to it.

Since Macy's Department Store opens at 5 P.M. on Thanksgiving Day, after we ate we marched two blocks to the store and waited in a line of humanity that wrapped around a city block. Once we got in the store, you couldn't stir them with a stick — bumping into you, rushing around and all. I'm not the Starbucks' kind but I saw one and told my entourage I was going to wait for them over there. I ordered something I couldn't pronounce and drank it down. My family finally gave me a reprieve.

By then we were hungry and ate at Olive Garden for our last supper in New York City. Yep, I know what you may be thinking. Olive Garden? By the third night we all were missing Olive Garden's salad, breadsticks, and never ending pasta bowl. I must admit that the cost of that meal was much more than what we spend for it Georgia. I guess it's because the Olive Garden in the Big Apple is further away from their headquarters in Orlando.

Speaking of food in New York City — my favorite eating place was a vendor set up across the street from our hotel. It's called Halal and it had the best lamb sandwich loaded with meat and it came with a soft drink. All for $5.50 cash money. Frankly, I could have eaten there every meal, and went down one night from our hotel just because I had a hankering for it.

On Friday, we took a scheduled tour of the 9-11 Memorial, Liberty Island, and a subway ride. Our guide was a fast-talking New Yorker that took us some time to get used to. He did an admirable job for the tour group. He even took us to one of the fire station houses who lost the majority of their firemen on 9-11. We read their names on that firehouse wall and remembered that day. Faye, Roxanne and I had been to the Statue of Liberty, but, it was a brand new experience for Madison. She thoroughly enjoyed it.

Red Britches at Jekyll Island

DURING MY TEENAGE YEARS, I WAS ASKED TO GO ALONG with a friend of mine on their church's annual youth trip to Jekyll Island, Georgia, off the Georgia coast. My friend had an acoustic guitar, we both wore those surf shirts that changed colors every time they were washed, and we sat and played and sang—me and him. Fortunately for us, that drew girls the same age as us. Later that evening, we went to the small fair-like venue near the beach and a girl from South Carolina began to talk to me. Up until that time, something like that had never happened to me. She asked me if I was one of the boys that were singing near the beach earlier that day, and I told her yes. She said she liked it a lot but really liked my red britches. The red britches I was wearing for that trip were size 29-inch waist and 31 inch length—a lean mean fighting machine, not really, but it sounds good.

Because of my red britches that night, the South Carolina girl and I talked for hours right there near the beach at Jekyll Island. I don't remember what we talked about, we just talked. Looking back on it, I should have asked for a kiss, but knowing me back then, I was scared to death. The only mouth kisses I had had up until that time was from my Big Mama Jenrette who always kissed her grandchildren right square on the mouth—snuff and all. I've never had another pair of red britches.

Sky Miles

THE TWO AND HALF YEARS IN BETWEEN MY MILITARY CA-
reer and federal civil service employment, I worked for the
Georgia Baptist Children's Home, the Georgia Department
of Corrections, and the dementia ward in a nursing home.
During those two and half years, I really missed working
with the military and jumped at the opportunity to work for
the Department of Defense once again, this time as a civil
service employee. My job was at the National Headquarters
for the Air Force Reserve located at Robins AFB, Georgia.
My role was as their Drug Demand Reduction Program
Manager, responsible for substance abuse prevention education and random drug testing at 66 military hospitals in 29
states.

Initially, that job took me to the friendly skies all over the
United States, all the while racking up Sky Miles from Delta
Airlines. After several months on the job, I never saw those
miles on the periodic pamphlet I'd receive from Delta, so, I
inquired. They told me they had been awarding my sky miles,
and I asked them to what address. They gave me my daddy's

address near Jacksonville, Florida. Unbeknownst to me, my daddy had been receiving my Sky Miles. I told the Delta representative on the other end of the phone line my actual address and asked her to fix it. She said she could not go back and retrieve those miles for me since they had been used.

I called my daddy and explained to him what had happened and he told me he didn't know where the Sky Miles were coming from, he was simply using them. He went to Germany on them. One of my sisters took a trip to Boston. So, because my daddy was Don Sr. and I am Don Jr. that is the reasoning behind why my Sky Miles got screwed up. A word to the wise, if your name ends in Sr., Jr., III, II, IV, make sure you get your own Sky Miles.

Walking Job Interview

EVERY MILITARY PERSON THAT CHOOSES TO MAKE THE SER-
vice a career has the customary "short tour" without family
members. Mine was the Republic of South Korea in 1988
and 1989. My job for the first few months was serving as
the base's Director of Base Administration, which entailed
oversight management of the Post Office, the Reprographics Office, the Publications Distribution Site, the Base Information Transfer Office, and Inspector General support. I
was also responsible for the supervision of a score of military
members and Korean Nationals.

Three months into my 12 month tour, a new base commander was selected. Customarily a new base commander
has his own staff, so, the colonel began his selection process.
It wound up being a walking job interview. The colonel was
looking for his Executive Officer to fulfill the roles of what
most know as an Executive Secretary in the civilian world.
I was one of several captains under his purview at the time.
The morning came when he came to my office areas to meet

and greet my fellow workers and, unbeknownst to me, conduct a walking job interview.

Frankly, I was not looking for the job as his new Executive Officer and proceeded to tell him how important my role was for the entire base of 5000 plus. During a part of our walking around, we passed by the men's latrine area and heard a loud gush of water coming from behind the door. The colonel was inquisitive and asked me what that noise was. I replied that once you've seen one military latrine, you've seen them all. He said he wanted to see anyway.

I walked in first. To my surprise, one of the Korean Nationals was taking his morning bath inside our deep sink, without a stitch of clothes on. Bear in mind that the deep sink is really not all that deep. His backside was exposed and the rest of his was body bent over, washing his feet. It was a sight to behold.

The colonel took one look and asked me where our next stop was to be. Keeping my military bearing and not cracking a smile or laughing aloud, we proceeded to the next area of the walking job interview. After the colonel left, I was mortified that he saw what he saw and knew I was in trouble.

The next morning, the colonel called me on the phone and told me I had another job. I thought I had been fired, however, he told me I would start working for him as his newly appointed Executive Officer the following day. I told him thank you and asked him two questions. The first was, "Who will do my current job?" Which he replied, "You will, Billy Bob." Yep, from then on when we had private conversations, he addressed me as Billy Bob.

The last question was, "What are my duty hours?" My colonel replied, "The B shift."

"The B shift," I replied.

He said, "Be at work before I arrive in the morning, and be at work when I leave at night."

Afterwards I met with all my subordinate supervisors and shared the news with them and told them I depended on them to run the show while I served as the base commander's Executive Officer. For the remainder of my short tour, I would spend a few hours weekly checking on my senior non-commissioned officer in charge and was pleasantly surprised that they performed their roles superbly, while I worked the B shift at the base headquarters building.

A few years ago, I looked up the name of my base commander and learned he retired in the Seattle area and had died of cancer in 2009. I found his obituary and it read that he had a long and distinguished military career as a pilot, logging more than 10,000 hours and counted his time as the Base Commander at Osan Air Base, Republic of South Korea, as his crowning glory. I hope in some way I helped him with that.

Ted Turner in the Flesh

ONE OF MY MILITARY TDYs TOOK ME TO A U.S. POSTAL Service conference in Atlanta, held at the Omni Hotel. One of my roles at Moody AFB, Valdosta, Georgia, was that of Postal Officer at the time. It was 1990. The afternoon I arrived, I met a fellow Postal Officer from another AF base and we took a walk through the cavernous Omni Hotel. Remembering that it was owned by Ted Turner, the media mogul, I mentioned to my new colleague that it would be something if we got to see Ted Turner in the flesh. Just as I said it, a gentleman with his back to us was waiting to board one of the elevators. This gentleman, apparently hearing what I said, turned around facing us, smiled a huge smile, then turned back around and boarded the elevator. Our wish came true that day, we got to see Ted Turner in the flesh.

Famous People

DURING MY NUMEROUS TDY TRIPS THROUGH U.S. AIR-
ports and hotels, I got to see with my own eyes some famous
people. While waiting for my plane in the San Francisco
airport, I saw Mohammed Ali, then Kareem Abdul Jabbar,
and then former U.S. Ambassador Andrew Young. During a
TDY to the Pentagon, I got to see Lynda Carter, of Wonder
Woman fame, and F. Lee Ermey, famous for his role as the
Marine Drill Sergeant in the movie *Full Metal Jacket*. Surprisingly to me, they both are taller than I thought.

Also, in the Atlanta airport, I met the one and only Her-
shel Walker, the Heisman Trophy winner from the University of Georgia. I also saw two famous people walking through
the Baltimore Washington International Airport—Lynda
Carter again, and Wolfman Jack, of radio fame and who
made a cameo appearance in the movie *American Graffiti*.
I also got to meet, shake hands with, and got a picture with
and a book on the history of UGA from the one and only
Coach Vince Dooley. And last, my wife and I, while I was
stationed at Fort Meade, Maryland, would go to the Veter-

ans Day Observance at Arlington National Cemetery each year. We saw then President Bill Clinton give a speech after laying a wreath at the Tomb of the Unknown Soldiers. You know, except for Coach Dooley, I forgot to get an autograph from any of them.

Must Have Slept Through that Class

OVER THE LAST SEVERAL YEARS, THE NATIONAL NEWS HAS been dotted with those who wear the military uniform and its medals erroneously—posing as war heroes. During my military boot camp during the Summer of 1971, each trainee was taught a lot of things relating to the military way of life. One of those was the classroom on the proper wear of military awards and decorations.

My first job in the Air Force after arriving at Robins AFB in Warner Robins, Georgia, was in the base mail room. Since the job involved the movement of mail throughout the sprawling complex, it required the wear of the utility uniform, or commonly referred to as "fatigues". The wear of fatigues does not require the wear of military decorations. However, the base military clothing sales office was located in between my barracks and the chow hall (now both are referred to as dormitories and dining facilities). One day after eating lunch, I stopped by the military clothing sales office and looked at the wall rack which held all the Air Force's military medals and associated ribbons. Since I had a few dollars on me, I picked out and paid for ten real pretty ones, because of the different colors in them and wore them to work the next day in my dress blue uniform.

I must have temporarily lost my mind because I had not earned any of them, but still had them on my chest for all my coworkers to see. I was proud of the way they looked on me. One of my coworkers, who also had one stripe on his sleeve, asked me about them and I told him I bought them at the military clothing sales office because they had many colors in them and that he could buy some, too.

He went missing for a few minutes until I heard him and our supervisor, a Senior Master Sergeant (with eight stripes on his sleeve), coming around the corner talking about my ribbons on my chest. Immediately I knew I was in trouble, so I quickly pulled them off my chest and stuck them in my pants pocket. If you know anything about military ribbons, you know they are affixed on the uniform's fabric by a series of sharp pins with clasps we commonly referred to as "frogs". Since the "frogs" were then inside the inner part of my uniform, the sharp pins were now digging through my pants legs, cutting my legs with every one of my movements.

My supervisor asked me why I was out of uniform and could readily tell by looking at my uniform the leftover pin holes where the ribbons use to be. He told me not to let that happen again. For all I know, I could have had the Congressional Medal of Honor on my chest that day. During the summer of 1971, I must have slept through the class on the proper wear of military medals and ribbons. I learned my lesson early and it never happened again.

Requisition Some Forms

First, some background information on my formative years of elementary and high school. I failed the first grade because my mama told me I fell in love with my first first-grade teacher. So, all the way through my remaining years in the Cook County, Georgia, public school system, I was a year behind those of my same age. I don't know if that had anything to do with my lack of knowledge regarding an extensive vocabulary or not.

One of my jobs in the Air Force was ensuring my fellow Airmen had the required forms to get the mission accomplished. As a matter of fact, there was a military form required to get a military form. I don't know which really came first. My supervisor came to my desk one day and asked me the following, "Airman, requisition some forms for me today, and here is the list." Frankly, I didn't know what "requisition" meant, but I was glad he left me a list. I got those forms for them that day.

Vest and All

ONE OF MY TDYs DURING THE YEAR OF 1978 WAS TO MIN-
neapolis, Minnesota, for three weeks, from the island of
Guam. The training was very extensive and taught me how
to effectively counsel the individual affected with alcohol
and/or drug addiction, and also his or her family members.
The training was held with fellow civilians, so we in the military were allowed to wear civilian clothes during the three
week training. After the TDY, I traveled back to Guam and
had telephoned my wife the flight number and the anticipated time of arrival at the Guam airport. She was waiting there
for me but did not recognize me. During the TDY I grew
out a beard — a three-week old beard. She told me later that
she didn't expect me to have a beard, but did notice a man
getting off the plane with a beard wearing a three-piece suit.
That man was me, vest and all.

It's a Small AF After All

During my time with the AF, I continually ran into folks who either knew my brothers, my uncles, or me from back in the day. Case in point, while conducting a newcomer's class at Maxwell AFB in Alabama, a Technical Sergeant came up to me after the first morning break and asked me if I knew a MSgt Joe Jenrette from Barksdale AFB, Louisiana. I told him he was one of my daddy's brothers. Also, while at Robins AFB, an NCO, after seeing my name tag, asked me if I knew an old man who owned and operated a saw mill near Baldwin, Florida, with my same last name. I told him it was my Big Daddy Jenrette, daddy's daddy.

Another story: a fellow church member was TDY to Langley AFB, Virginia, and met my brother, MSgt Scott Jenrette. He said Scott was briefing them on a revised supply procedure the AF was beginning to use.

Another story: during my last assignment as a civilian at Robins, the colonel in charge of the AF Reserve Information Technology Directorate called me on the telephone and asked me if I knew Lt Colonel Brian Jenrette. I told him he is my brother and was then stationed in Colorado where he retired. The colonel told me they worked together in the same office at the Pentagon several years back. It is a small world after all—and that's not only a ride at the Magic Kingdom in Orlando.

Weathering the Hurricane

THE YEAR WAS 1985, THE PLACE WAS KEESLER AFB, Mississippi, the time of year was Labor Day weekend. My wife and I, along with our three children, weathered Hurricane Elena inside one of the three-story block built school houses on base. The storm initially was headed to hit the Mississippi Gulf Coast on the Saturday or Sunday of that Labor Day weekend. However, it stalled and headed for the Florida west coast for several hours, then turned back stronger and eventually hit where we were late Sunday night. The Hurricane was a category 3 with winds clocked at 133 miles per hour, and made a direct hit east of our location at Dauphin Island, Alabama.

Eventually we learned that 13,000 homes were damaged and 200 homes destroyed by the hurricane. Since I was a First Lieutenant at the time, I was placed in charge of the bottom floor of the building. That meant I was to ensure law and order and some semblance of cleanliness. That was extremely difficult since we got into the building on Saturday afternoon and were not allowed to leave until late Monday,

Labor Day 1985. When my family and I finally left the safe haven, we approached our car and fortunately it only had some scratches and the like. However, some of the vehicles right next to ours had busted out windows and a lot of exterior damage from flying debris.

When the all clear was given for us to go back to our home, it was like driving through where a bomb had been set off. Frankly, we prepared ourselves for the worst. Fortunately, our home was not damaged, just no electricity, for four long days. The neighbor behind our home had a large pine tree fall through their kitchen. Because we had no electricity, we ate what was in our freezers — steaks, hamburgers, pork chops, ham, and the like. Neighbors for blocks would set up their barbeque grills and we would eat real good.

Fortunately, the water remained working in our neighborhood so we had potable water for drinking and for other necessary sanitary uses. Because of my actions (or work in charge of the first floor) I was awarded the Humanitarian Service Medal later that year. I didn't expect it nor did I do that work to be recognized. I did what I did because we had to survive — and we did. Every Labor Day Weekend I remember that Labor Day Weekend a long time ago. But it really doesn't seem that long ago.

Summer Vacations at the Pea Patch

BEFORE I RECEIVED MY COMMISSIONING AS A SECOND LIEU-
tenant, I was never bothered by those letters and phone calls
asking that we attend a free three day, two night vacation in
beautiful sunny Florida. For some reason, folks thought we
had hit the lottery or something just by putting on those
"butter bars". We fell for it, and so did some friends of ours,
all going to the same location and same time share venue.
We all traveled in separate vehicles, checked in, and learned
we had to sit in on a "quick" 90-minute presentation about
the place where we were staying. We did not have the option
of refusing. My friend Walt, his family, and my wife and I
and our family prepared for the presentation.

The first thing they did was take our children away to
play video games and the like. Then they separated families, however, prior to going in, Walt gave me some great
advice—don't buy a thing! Tell them the truth when they
ask you where you usually go on family vacations. So, I remembered what my friend told me. My wife and I were met
by an older gentleman with a New York accent who talked

extremely too fast for both of us. But we let him talk. As best I can remember, he was the first man I ever saw that wore earrings, in both ears. Remember, this was in the mid-1980s.

"Don't buy a thing" continually rang in my ears, the advice given by my friend to the fast talker before us. Then the fast talker asked where we usually spent our family vacations, and I told him the truth. I responded, "The Pea Patch".

To which the fast talker asked, "I'm not familiar with that resort location, where is it." It was then that I continued to tell him the truth and told him the pea patch was located beside my in-law's home. He was intrigued and asked how long my in-laws had lived at that location. I told him since 1963. He seemed impressed until I told him the things we did at the pea patch. I told him that we continually bend over and pick peas from the ground, place them into buckets, then take them into the home and shell them, blanch them, and then we can them for the winter.

At that, the man asked me if I had any questions about the property and I told him no. There was also a gift offered to each couple after successfully completing the sales pitch by the fast talker. It was a choice between a $50 meal voucher at a local eatery or Disney Dollars, good for use at any of the Disney parks. We asked for the Disney Dollars and used them to pay for $5 ice creams and $3.50 soft drinks.

My friend and his wife were waiting for us when we came out of the fast talker's office. Walking away, I told him I had followed his instructions to the letter. I don't know who was happier for that sales pitch to be over—my wife and me, or the fast talker. Since then we are extremely leery of fast talking sales pitches, for that matter, even slow talking sales pitches.

Box of Band-Aids

I AM NOT A FIXER-UPPER, NEVER HAVE BEEN, NEVER WILL be. While assigned to the AF base in Biloxi, Mississippi in the early to mid-1980s, our children were all pre-teens. My wife and I purchased a swing set and my job, as the dad, was to put it together. Good luck on that one.

After getting the large box home and its contents strewed over our backyard, I began to assemble it. Probably one of my mistakes in attempting to build objects is not following those directions that come in the box. You know the ones I'm talking about. They're written in English, then in Spanish, and I still don't know what language the other ones are.

As I continued to build it, I started to notice what looked like red blotches on some of the pieces. Then to my surprise, I learned it was my own blood. I had cut my fingers all up in the process of building my children's swing set. As fate would have it, it was near my birthday and some friends of ours came over later to wish me happy birthday. Learning of my futile attempt to build the swing set, which was nowhere near finished, my friend Walt and his wife, Darlene, gave me a wrapped gift. Upon opening it, I learned it was a giant box of band-aids—just for me.

Fortunately, my friend Walt was and still is a great handy man and "helped" me finish building my children's swing set. Thank God for good friends and band-aids.

Can't See

SUPERMAN, THE MOVIE, THE ONE WITH THE LATE CHRISTO-
pher Reeve in the title role, came out while we were living
on the Island of Guam. Expectedly, when my wife and I got
to the base theatre for the first showing of the movie, it was
packed — so much so we had to sit separately in the theatre.
While walking to our car in the theatre parking lot after the
movie, I asked my wife why the screen was so blurry. She said
it wasn't. Oops, I then knew it was my eye sight. I was only
27. Immediately I remembered my childhood friends that
wore eye glasses and we used to call them "four eyes". Well,
it was my time.

The next duty day, I got an appointment with the optometrist and took the eye test and learned that I needed glasses.
They measured them for me and in a few days issued what
were commonly referred to back then as BCGs. That stood
for birth control glasses. That meant that they were so ugly
no one of the opposite sex would want to be seen around you
looking like that. But I put them on.

My office building was across a field from the optometrist's office so I proceeded to walk across it—with my BCGs and new eye sight. I received no advance warning. It was a whole new world out there. I could see again. However, looking down at my feet hitting the ground, I had the sensation that I was stepping out like a mule in a briar patch. I don't know if you've ever seen that, but that was how I looked. But I could see. Oh, our second daughter was born on the Island of Guam the next year.

Rent-a-Family

WHILE ASSIGNED AT CHANUTE AFB, ILLINOIS, OUTSIDE the hamlet of Rantoul, I was selected for military jury duty. An airman had been caught red-handed stealing fellow airmen's personal belongings — a no-no in military environs. I was one of 12 jury members, all fellow commissioned officers. In the military court room sat the defendant and his defense attorney; and behind them was an older man and woman. We, the jury, noticed that the woman from time to time during the trial would sob when certain testimony was given by those who had been the brunt of theft.

Eventually, we found the airman guilty of all charges, however, one of the jury member's heart strings were pulled every time the woman would sob. Since Chanute AFB was a technical training base responsible for the training and education of new recruits, it was easier to discharge an airman with less than six months of military service. The airman in question received a discharge and sent back home.

After my duty as a jury member was over, I saw the defense attorney at the base gymnasium days later and asked him about the airman's mother and father that were sitting behind him during the trial. At first the attorney was reluctant to respond to my inquiry, however, he told me the man and woman were not his parents.

Apparently, the airman had hired the older couple to sit behind him and appear to be someone very close to him. That ploy worked on one jury member, but not the remaining 11 of us. Rent-a-Family—just when you thought you'd heard it all.

I Think I Might Have Killed Him

FRATERNIZATION IS NOT A NEW THING IN THE MILITARY. We had problems with it in the 1980s, too. At one of my military assignments, we were responsible for the morale, welfare, and housing of new recruits while they received formal training and education for their new AF career. I had 12 permanent party airmen responsible for ensuring that the airmen received that military training and education.

Each airman was taught that fraternization was a no-no. One of my airmen stepped out of line regarding fraternization and I called him "on the carpet". "On the carpet" in military speak means that you have to stand before the commanding officer's desk, formally report in, and learn what the charges are against him or her.

The airman in question allegedly had been fraternizing with the younger female airmen on more than one occasion. As was the custom, I had my first sergeant in my office when I called anyone on the carpet, and this was no different. Once the airman in question came in, he was extremely casual instead of the customary reporting in to a military commander.

After experiencing his casual demeanor, I ordered him to report in, to which he got pale as a ghost.

Then I began reading the charges to him and his Rights of Advisement. Of course, I had received the okay from the local JAG Office to proceed with the event. As I continued to read the charges, I looked up and the airman in question was not there, and neither was my first sergeant. They were both on the floor. Apparently, the Airman in question had fainted and my first sergeant was administering aide to him. My first response was: "I think I might have killed him!"

Fortunately, after one night in the local military hospital he was released and to my knowledge he never, ever fraternized with any of the younger troops.

A Bad Mouth

Growing up in the small South Georgia town of Adel with two sisters and my maternal grandmother who raised us after our mama died, included no medical or dental insurance. So, when we had a toothache, the home remedy was to place an aspirin in the affected tooth or to smoke a cigarette. I never liked cigarettes nor the smoke from them so I went the route of aspirin use. It would numb the pain some but I can remember many nights crying myself to sleep from severe tooth pain.

When I turned 20, I went into the Air Force and all that changed. As was the custom back in 1971, for anyone living in South Georgia going in to the military, you had to go down to the Military Examining and Process Center in Jacksonville, Florida. A part of the process included a dentist and dental technicians thorough review of each prospective recruit's mouth and the teeth within.

When it came to my time, after the technician saw my mouth he called over the team of dentists there and I heard him tell them, "Now that's a bad mouth." What they found were three abscessed teeth, so bad that sores had developed above each. Fortunately for me, they cleared me for entry into the Air Force and months later after finishing boot camp and arrival at my first duty station, I had many visits to the local dentist's office. They fixed my teeth and now where those abscessed teeth used to be are three permanent bridges. Thank God for the Air Force pill.

DAWG

During my Korea assignment in 1988 and 1989, I kept myself busy since I was there without my family. I did some officiating of basketball and football, and I ran each Sunday with the Hash Harriers and Hounds. If you are a runner, you may be familiar with the HHHs. For you who are not, here goes.

The Hash Harriers are the rabbits who spread a trail of white flour on a running course and the Hounds are the runners following in behind. There are customarily two rabbits, one who goes the correct route, and the other takes you the incorrect way. The hounds who go the incorrect route learn later because that rabbit places a symbol on the trail telling them it's the incorrect path. Some of the runs would last over an hour and provided a way to see the South Korean countryside not afforded in other ways.

After the 12th run, your fellow Hounds would give you a HHH nickname. The Hounds would take into consideration what they knew about the runner. They bequeathed the following nickname for me: DAWG! How appropriate.

Go Get Your Eyeglasses Now

WHILE STATIONED IN SOUTH KOREA IN THE LATE 1980s I was responsible for all things administrative for over 5000 AF members. One of those roles was the reprographics support, or making paper copies of originals. One day a CMSgt came to my office, concerned over a copier order he had just picked up. I took a look at it and saw that most pages of the document were not readable.

My junior NCO responsible for proofreading every reprographics job was there as usual, so I called for him to come to my office so we could talk about the issue. When he arrived at my office, he bumped into the doorway and had difficulty finding a chair to sit in. I immediately noticed he was not wearing his eyeglasses and asked him where they were. He then asked what the issue was and he said he would rectify it. I again asked him where his eyeglasses where. He told me I didn't need to know. I told him to tell me.

He told me he left them in a hurry the night before at his girlfriend's home right outside the AF base. I told him to go get them and that he had 15 minutes to get them and to get back here. He then told me he feared for his life if he went back there. Apparently, his girlfriend had more than one boyfriend and one of them showed up while they were together and my junior NCO said he had to run for his life, thereby leaving his eyeglasses and some of his clothes.

I then ordered him to get some eyeglasses within the hour and correct the wrong for CMSgt's copier order. You can't make up some of this stuff.

You Better Leave

THE SAME JUNIOR NCO IN THE AFOREMENTIONED STORY got into more hot water while under my supervision and management. As was the custom when a newly assigned AF member came to work for me, we would take him or her to one of the local Korean Restaurants for what we referred to as a "Green Bean". It was also customary to wear civilian clothes to these gatherings.

The day my junior NCO arrived, we took him for a Green Bean. Our Superintendent, an AF CMSgt, was married to a Korean National, and was extremely protective of her. Everyone knew not to approach her for a dance or a cocktail — everyone except the newly assigned junior NCO. While our CMSgt went to the restroom, we saw the unspeakable — the junior NCO started hitting on the CMSgt's wife.

It appeared at first that she went along with it since it had been a long time since she had gotten that kind of attention from someone other than her husband. I had not noticed what was going on until one of my other airmen came to me and told me what was happening. I immediately went to the junior NCO, warning him that the woman's husband was extremely jealous and that he would be back from the restroom soon. He ignored my warning, "You Better Leave".

At that moment, our CMSgt came back to the table where his wife and the junior NCO were seated with his left arm around her neck. The CMSgt was livid and told the junior NCO to get up from the table and leave. He did so.

This occurred about three months into my twelve month tour in Korea and I found myself trying to protect the junior NCO from our CMSgt. I'm not sure what happened after I left, but I did brief the Captain who relieved me what happened. For some reason, I don't think the junior NCO ever learned his lesson.

Thanksgiving Dinner 1978

FROM 1978 TO 1980, MY WIFE AND I LIVED ON THE ISLAND of Guam. It was my second military assignment of what would eventually be nine military bases in a 24 year AF career. When I first received my orders for Guam, I looked for it on the map — in the Caribbean. It wasn't there. Then I got out the Encyclopedia Britannica and learned that it was in the South Pacific, near the Philippine Islands, a long way from the Caribbean and from Robins AFB, Georgia.

After arriving on the island, Faye and I began looking for a place to worship God and grow closer to him since we were then over 8,000 miles from our Georgia roots. We eventually would attend a small congregation of fellow military members and their families in the village of Yigo (pronounced Jigo). Our pastor and his wife were from way out west and we grew to love them and grew spiritually under their watch and care.

When Thanksgiving rolled around, they invited the military service members and their families over to one of the sailor's home for Thanksgiving Dinner. That Thanksgiving morning, I slept in and before we left home for theirs, Faye asked me if I wanted breakfast before we left. Since it was nearly 11 a.m. I told her no. I wish I hadn't.

We arrived at our friends home around 11:20, thinking it would only be 40 minutes or so before we ate our dinner. Well, 12 noon came and went. Then 1 P.M. came and went. Then 2 P.M. came and went. My stomach was really growling by then. Then 3 P.M. Then 4 P.M. Then 5 P.M.

Then finally at 6 P.M. we had Thanksgiving Dinner. I was famished! And the meal was so good!! After the meal, I told everyone there that the meal was fantastic and asked why we had it for supper instead of for dinner.

They told us where they were from, and that their Thanksgiving Dinner is always the evening meal. Got it! Needless to say, prior to our second and last Thanksgiving Dinner on Guam, I had a full breakfast before leaving home.

Carry Her to the Doctor

OUR SECOND DAUGHTER, VELMA ROXANNE JENRETTE, WAS born on Guam in May 1979. Several months before her birth, I was tapped for some temporary military assignments taking me away from Faye for a period of time. I asked our pastor and his wife if they would look after Faye while I was out of pocket. They gracefully agreed. Faye and I asked them to carry her to the doctor's office and any other trips she deemed necessary. Our pastor and his wife were perplexed at our request to "carry" Faye to the doctor and then told us they would be happy to "give her a ride" to the doctor's office not to "carry" her. They say tomato, I say mater.

A Fair Trade

DURING MY FORMATIVE YEARS GROWING UP IN THE Housing Projects in Adel, Georgia, I learned a great deal about things. Since most housing projects have a lot of sidewalks, I became intimate with most of those sidewalks around our apartment. I think I learned how to ride a bicycle by myself there and you can imagine how many times I fell off of it and scraped my legs, knees, elbows, etc.

One day as I was walking by Connie G's apartment where she, her mama, and two siblings lived, I noticed she had a brown looking medicine bottle that she was pouring onto one the scrapes she had on her knee. And I watched it boil out stuff I had never seen before. I stood amazed! I asked her if I could try some. Connie said I could have the whole bottle in exchange for something of mine. The only thing I had with me was my bicycle and I wasn't going to exchange that for the bottle with some hydrogen peroxide in it.

I went back home where mama was cutting chicken up to fry for that night's supper. And customarily, she would always take her rings off and place them on the window sill.

I seized the opportunity when mama wasn't looking. Once I exchanged the rings for the hydrogen peroxide bottle with Connie G, I proceeded to pour the liquid on every part of me that I could remember had ever been scrapped—and it did its thing, too.

Everything was going along good until at our screen door Connie's mama knocked. When mama answered the door, Ms. G asked her if she was missing her rings and mama, after looking on the window sill, saw they were not there and replied yes. About that time, I made myself scarce from anywhere near the door screen, because I knew what was coming from my mama.

After Ms. G returned Mama's rings to her, I thought Ms. G would take my bottle of hydrogen peroxide, but she didn't. It didn't take me long to deplete its contents.

Passing Georgia History

DURING THE TIME I WENT TO THE GEORGIA PUBLIC SCHOOL system in Cook County, Georgia, there was an academic requirement that each child in the 8th grade had to take and pass a class on Georgia history. Usually I was good in history but that school year my mama died and my heart and my mind was not on doing my school homework or what we commonly referred to as "lessons".

One teacher, Mr. R, was the sole educator for this class. As I best recollect, I remember him teaching us about James Oglethorpe, the Trail of Tears, and the War of Jenkins Ear—and that's most of what I got out of it. The last week of that school year, after one of the Georgia history classes, Mr. R asked me, Johnny R, and Donald B, to remain behind for a few minutes. He had a proposition for us three. He told us that out of the entire 8th class, 150+ students, we three lacked the passing grade of at least 70.

I asked how close I was and he told me I had a 67; I don't know how far off Johnny and Donald were from the 70 mark. Then Mr. R threw out the proposition that would never do in today's "time-out in the corner" world—he said if each us would receive 10 licks from his paddle, he would give us enough points to pass his Georgia history class. Thinking back on it, he probably would have passed us anyway because he really didn't want us boys back in his classroom another year and a head taller than the incoming 8th graders. So, we agreed and I went first.

He asked me how many I wanted the first day and I told him four licks, and three licks the next day, and the last three licks the last day of school. If I had it to do over, I would have chosen to have all ten licks that first day, because after the second lick it all went numb. Someone asked me a while back how long it's been since I've visited Six Flags over Georgia amusement park, I replied to them, "When it was called Two Flags". I think Mr. R would be proud of me.

First Grade, the First Time

IN 1957, I WAS IN THE FIRST GRADE THE FIRST TIME. As I recollect, my teacher was beautiful and mama told me after I asked what contributed to my failing the first grade, told me I fell in love with my teacher. And, how did I pass the first grade the second time?

First Grade, the Second Time

In 1958, I repeated the first grade and Ms. Delle B, the principal of Adel Elementary, in her infinite wisdom, gave me a teacher that didn't look anything like my first one—so I passed the second time.

Second Grade

WHEN I FINALLY MADE IT TO THE SECOND GRADE, OUR teacher made each of us go to the chalk board and write the name that we go by. So, I wrote the following: Donny Behave. She didn't find that humorous at all. I just wrote what she asked me to, that was the name I went by.

Fried Chicken Healing

DURING MY 24 YEARS SERVING IN THE AF, MY FAVORITE location was Biloxi, Mississippi, before the casinos came in. Many years after being stationed there, we went back to visit our life-long friends who lived in nearby Ocean Springs. During one visit, we went to the local fried chicken restaurant to eat some of that good tasting yard bird. Unfortunately, when I was getting out of my car my son, then eight years old, mistakenly shut the car door on my left hand, fracturing my pinky finger. Even though it caused tremendous pain, I ate my chicken but the pain got worse.

When we got back to our friend's home, I took some Tylenol to hopefully ease the pain. I've always been one with a low tolerance for meds and for pain, and once I took that medicine it knocked me out cold. My wife told me I was asleep in less than 10-15 minutes but to me it seemed like a full night's rest. I attribute that good sleep to that fried chicken from the Ocean Springs restaurant.

Red VW

My father-in-law was a VW car mechanic extraordinaire. That was his specialty. One evening while assisting him with handing him the right socket wrenches, etc. in his workplace garage, a VW Beetle came up his long driveway. My father-in-law was under the VW he was working on perched on his creeper, so I told him a VW was coming up the driveway, to which he replied, "It's a red one, ain't it?" To which I replied, "Yes sir." I was amazed that he knew the sound of VWs so well that he could tell what color they were without even seeing them. Years later, when I shared this story with another older gentleman and my father-in-law overheard our conversation, he then told that he could see the VW that night from his vantage point on the creeper. And I thought he was that good at telling the colors of VWs by the way they sounded.

Back it Up

WHEN MY BOY WAS 10 OR 11 YEARS OLD, HE WENT TO THE local barbeque joint in Hawkinsville, Georgia, with his Papa Brown driving his pickup truck (old blue). The way my son tells it is as follows: my son was driving shotgun while his Papa ordered the takeout sandwiches from the squawk box and then proceeded to the pay window. He said after his Papa paid for the sandwiches at the pay window, he commenced to driving out of the parking lot and on to the highway, without stopping at the carryout window. Before pulling on to the highway, my son said he told his Papa that they didn't get their sandwiches. Expecting his Papa to drive around the joint and go in to get the sandwiches, Papa did the following: he proceeded to back up old blue all the way to the takeout window. I asked my son what was the response from other customers waiting for their sandwiches after paying at the appropriate window. He said he heard one of the patrons, after seeing Papa backing up toward their front end of their vehicle, say, "Back it up, there comes Mr. Brown!" And they all did, every vehicle in line during that summer day. Such are the goings on of a small town.

The Ruler is Wrong

HERE'S ANOTHER STORY ABOUT MY PA-IN-LAW. SINCE HE and my mother-in-law had a wood burning stove that helped to heat their home, he kept a lot of firewood ready to lug in to feed that stove. Needing some tin to place over his firewood pile to keep the wood from getting wet, the two of us went to the local home supply store looking for a piece of tin. For me - any piece of tin would have done the trick as long as it adequately covered the firewood—but not my pa-in-law. We went directly to the area where they had precut pieces of tin and we found tin about 3-4 feet wide and 10 feet long. Well, my pa-in-law, asked for some assistance and the young man told him that the tin we were looking at was precut to 10-foot long pieces. My pa-in-law disagreed with him. At that the store man called a fellow worker over to help him place that piece of tin closer to them and he commenced to measure the piece with a ruler. After measuring, they told my pa-in-law that it indeed did measure 10 feet, at which my pa-in-law responded, "Your ruler is wrong." And he walked away.

Paying it Forward

As a boy, I grew up in the housing projects in Adel, Georgia. One of my older friends in those projects was an old woman we called Granny S. As I recall, she was lady that was about as big around as she was tall and very much a Christian. When I would come to her screen door to say hello, she would invite me in and she would talk all things Jesus. Every summer one of her grandsons, named Kenny, would come to visit for several weeks from a faraway land called Warner Robins, Georgia. Even though it was a scant 100 miles away, for me and my family, it might have well been a million miles away. Case in point, no one in my immediate family knew how to drive nor owned a motorized vehicle. Kenny and I would play out in the woods behind the housing projects for weeks that turned into months that turned in to several years in a row. We played Cowboys and Indians and Tarzan, and Army, ever what struck our fancy that given day. After living in those projects for several years, my Grandma Smith bought us a Jim Walter Home and had it built on some land she previously had a home on that burned to the ground many years before. So, I lost touch with Granny S and my boyhood friend Kenny. Years later, I heard our insurance man tell my Ma Smith that Granny S had passed away. I cried. In 1995, my immediate family moved to Houston County after completing 24 years of military service in the Air Force. My daughter, Roxanne, started her junior year at Houston County High School. Early in that school year she shared with me and our family at the supper table that a girl named Jessie had reached out to her and they became friends. Well, when Jessie came to visit at our home I asked her what her last name was—and she said S-----. I shared the story of a boy named Kenny who used to come for the summers to spend time with his Granny S. It was the same Granny S that I talked about earlier in this story. Again, it's a small world, and that's not only a ride at Disney World. Even in death, Granny S' prayers are being answered.

Telephone Party Lines

As a boy growing up in the small rural South Georgia town of Adel, our home had a telephone party line. Everyone who had a phone back then was given information on what their telephone rings were. Ours was two long and one short ring and we knew to pick up the phone. We were on the party line with an elderly couple who lived kitty corner from us. They were Mr. and Mrs. McD. He worked at the cotton mill in Tifton and I earned my lunch money washing their automobile every Saturday. My Ma Smith, who raised me and my sisters after our mama died, was a widow woman for 33 years. During that time, she had many suitors, too numerous to count. One afternoon our phone rang the two long and one short ring and Ma answered it. One of her suitors was on the other end. And, as I recollect, Mrs. McD would join in to hear those conversations. Well, one day during a phone conversation with one of her suitors, Ma got tired of hearing Mrs. McD's hard breathing on the party line and she called her game. Ma said, "Mrs. McD, I know that's you on the other end listening to us?" To which Mrs. McD replied, "No I ain't!" Busted.

I Know My Daddy

SEVERAL YEARS BEFORE MY DADDY PASSED AWAY, ONE DAY after his 75th birthday, he was hospitalized for respiratory issues. He would die from mesothelioma—extreme exposure to asbestos on the Navy ships he served on for 21 years. Again, several years before his passing my wife and I went to visit him in the Orange Park, Florida hospital. The entire family was told to visit him because the medical folks were not sure if he would make it through. After we parked our car in the hospital parking lot, we ran up on one of Daddy's old Navy buddies, D. He saw us first and said he was there to visit my daddy, too. Well, we followed the instructions from family members who were already there with my daddy—Cardiac Intensive Care Unit (CICU). Upon entering the floor where the CICU was located we had to pick up a telephone right outside that unit to gain access to where my daddy's room was. After the three of us gained access, we went to the first room and there was my daddy, with no body in the room with him. It had been a few months seen I'd seen him and was shocked that he had an oxygen mask on his face and he couldn't talk. D and I went over to console my daddy. He looked so pale and could only respond to us by the rapid movement of his eyes upon ours. D began to stroke my daddy's hair and addressed him by his nickname—Shakey. I bent over his face and kissed him on the forehead. Faye, my wife, chose to remain at the entrance to that hospital room, and surprisingly told me and D that according to the name on the outside of that hospital room, that was not my daddy. I immediately told my wife that I knew the man before us was my daddy. Well, D, not convinced, went to the doorway and after reading also told me, "Donny, that's not your daddy!" D and I were embarrassed for our blunder and slowly backed our way out. We finally found my daddy with my stepmother and sister already by his bedside. Faye told Daddy what had happened and he replied, speaking about the blunder, "What are we going to do with him, Faye?" I'm not through with this story. Two of my younger brothers were flying in from their homes to be with daddy at the hospital, too, and we started worrying about their whereabouts since they called nearly two hours after arriving at the Jacksonville International Airport. Well, they finally made it to Daddy's room. They told us they had spent the last 45 minutes in the first room after entry into the CICU. That's the same room and the same little man. My brothers said they were kissing his forehead and talking to him, too. Then they both realized that wasn't our daddy. And they, too, backed their way out of that room. I can't fathom what was going on in that little man's head that day.

At least we gave him our time and concern. Hey, you can't make this stuff up.

Starting Line-Up

IN HIGH SCHOOL, I RAN TRACK AND PLAYED BASKETBALL. IT was customary before each basketball game that the announcer would give the names, position, and height and grade standing. I don't know why to this day, but they would announce the first letter of the player's first name and then his last name. I wish I had a nickel for every time my last name has been mispronounced—it's J-E-N-R-E-T-T-E, just like the girl's name Jeannett, but pronounced Jenrette. My senior year I finally got to be one of the starting five players and the first game at home the announcer mispronounced my last name. He pronounced it Jenerette. So, this is how it went that Tuesday night—"Starting at forward, 150 pounds, 6 foot 1 inch senior, D. Jenerette!" Well, the entire gym roared with laughter. It made me look down at my uniform to make sure everything was on properly. After the game, I asked our team manager, a fellow classmate, why the fans in the gym laughed after the announcer said my name. He laughed and explained to me that the way it came out was that I was a degenerate. Since my vocabulary was weak,

I asked him what that meant. He simply said, "Look it up in the dictionary." And I did. I started in 16 games that year.

Big Mama's House

MY DADDY'S MAMA WAS AFFECTIONATELY ADDRESSED BY her 46 grandchildren as Big Mama. It was not because of her physical stature, she was about 5-foot tall and slight of build. She was Big Mama because what she said went. That's Southern speak for the main most one, the Mac Mama, the Big Cheese. She shared a home with the county's attorney, Mr. C, or Colonel C. It was his home and about a fourth of it was uninhabitable because of the rotten wooden flooring. Oh, and it didn't have an indoor bathroom either. For me and my sister, who visited every weekend, we thought it a novelty to have to go out to the outhouse to do our business - until cold weather hit. When it got too cold, Big Mama would place a slop jar up under a wicket chair, cut a huge hole out of the seat of that chair and that's what we would use. The slop jar was not emptied until it was full and you didn't have to remember to take the top off the slop jar but once. One of the things Big Mama told us not to do was walk out too far on her large front porch. Well, at the ripe old age of 10, I tried it. I fell through the porch and didn't know I was really hurt until the kin folks who were there pulled me back up on the porch. I had cut a huge chunk out of my leg, just below my left knee cap. Fortunately, Moody AFB was only a 20-minute drive. The AF surgeon took me in and it took 50 stitches on the inside of the wound and 50 stitches on the outside and 10 days in the hospital. The rest of the Summer of 1961 was spent on crutches. Every time I see someone with crutches today, I remember not obeying my Big Mama that Saturday afternoon. After that I obeyed everything she said.

Kenny L

MY DAUGHTER, ROXANNE, WAS DRIVING HER FRIEND, JESSIE, home from school one afternoon and ran into a mail box, knocking it down. Being raised right, Roxanne went to the door of the home and when no one answered the phone she left a note on how to contact me to make it right. Well, I got the call and it was a man we'll call Kenny L to protect the innocent or the guilty. He proceeded, in his broken English, what kind of new mail box he wanted and that he wanted it placed in a different location than his old one. Since I've never been a handy man, I asked my friend David, the builder of my home, to assist. And he did. Since we had to order the new mail box from Texas, the wait for it increased from days to weeks. And Kenny L was growing extremely impatient because he was thinking that I was backing out of the obligation to place a new mail box. During many phone conversations, I tried my best to persuade Kenny L that the mail box was on its way. Finally, it arrived and the day we were to place it in the new location, I got to his home later than anticipated. At that time, I worked in the Prison Ministry at the Hawkinsville, Georgia location, which took me 20-25 minutes to get from point A to point B. Once I arrived at Kenny L's home, he was upset that it took me as long as it did. I told how long I had to travel and after seeing my Robins AFB sticker on my vehicle, he assumed I worked at Robins AFB and was telling him an untruth about it taking me as long as it did to place his new mailbox in the ground, where he wanted it. I got upset then and my friend David could sense it, too, so he placed the mailbox in the ground very quickly and we went on our way. Later that night, I answered the home phone and it was Kenny L. He proceeded to tell how disappointed he was in my getting his new mail box to him and in the ground, to which I began losing my religion, if you know what I mean. I got so angry I hung up on Kenny L. A minute later, David called me on my home phone, apologizing that he got me upset over the mailbox saga. It was David who pulled a prank on me a few minutes before. I apologized, too. After that, I told Roxanne that if she knocked down any more mailboxes, to be careful whose mailbox she knocked down.

Fused Tail Bone

MY LAST THREE YEARS OF MILITARY SERVICE I TRAVELED more temporary duty assignments (TDYs) than the previous 21 years altogether. My role as the Deputy Inspector General required me to visit and inspect the procedures at 32 Defense Courier Service stations located around the world. One such TDY was two and a half weeks away from my family and our townhouse located on Fort Meade, Maryland. That townhouse had two flights of stairs which separated the bedrooms with our sitting rooms downstairs. Once home, and in between another TDY after the weekend, I had to get up and go to the bathroom and mistakenly fell down the two flights of stairs. Ouch! Thinking back on it, I was either sleep walking or had forgotten I wasn't in a faraway hotel room, or both. At the time, I slept in my birthday suit. My commotion resulted in waking up the entire household, to include my two younger children, Roxanne, in her early teens, and Edwin, a preteen at the time. And they saw me at the bottom of the stairs with my feet over my head. Well, it hurt me so badly I jumped up and went back to bed. That next day I was picked up by my boss and we drove up to McGuire AFB, New Jersey, on an inspection trip together. That bed was the hardest bed I've slept on! Less than three years later, while undergoing my retirement physical and before leaving the military for good, the medical staff showed me X-rays of my body and the doctor pointed out to me that my tail bone had fused back together nicely. I didn't even know I had broken it during that fall.

Valid Driver's License

As I have mentioned, my vocabulary growing up was lacking. My last job before going into the military was working at a shirt factory for some Jewish gentlemen where I served as their Shipping Clerk. One day after the transfer company had already left with its daily pickup, we learned we had another shipment that had to be shipped that same day. So, my boss asked me to do it, with one caveat. Mr. Sol asked me if I had a valid driver's license. To which I replied, "I don't know if they're valid or not, but they're good." I delivered that shipment to the carrier located in Tifton, a 20-minute trip north—using my valid driver's license.

Hanging Tobacco

ONE OF MY SUMMER JOBS GROWING UP IN RURAL SOUTH Georgia was working in the hot tobacco fields. After we gathered up a day's worth of tobacco, we were required to hang it up on sticks which rested on logs used to perch the tobacco while it was flue cured. The early morning tobacco always had dew on it from the overnight dew that would fall, making that tobacco very wet. That dampness would turn in to a treacherous journey up the tobacco barn and its logs which were designed to hold the sticks of sewn in tobacco. As it turned out, I was duly elected to be the man with the highest perch up in the barns because they said I had the longest arms (and extremely gullible at that time). Well, the wet logs that evening were so slick that I lost my footing and fell, straddling one of the logs, injuring my private parts. It hurt me so bad that I lay in my bed at home for a few days to recuperate. We very rarely went to the doctor or a hospital, and this was no exception. Thank God it was not bad enough to prevent me from being the daddy to three wonderful children.

Popping a Sweat

BACK IN THE EARLY 1990S, MY BROTHER SCOTT AND I TOOK leave from our AF jobs to spend time together with our daddy. Daddy had been placed in the hospital with some respiratory issues so Scott and I decided to take care of some of the household chores Daddy usually handled. One of them was lawn care. At my daddy's home, they had Saint Augustine grass, known for its thick and deep blades of grass. Since it was a hot summer day, and I am the oldest of daddy's children, I directed Scott to take care of the front lawn and I would wait for him in the family swimming pool until he came around to the back lawn. Well, in what I thought would only take him 45 minutes, tops, it approached well over an hour. So, I got out of the pool and to my amazement, witnessed my brother attempting to push daddy's lawn mower over the thick grass ahead of him. And he was popping a sweat. After asking him to cut the mower off he told me, "No wonder Dad's having breathing problems, having to push this lawn mower!" I asked Scott to crank up the mower one more time. He did and at that I pulled a lever located on the right side of the mower's upper handle and engaged the motor-propelled lawn mower. He was attempting to mow daddy's lawn "self-propelled".

Do Something with that Cup

DURING MY LAST MILITARY ASSIGNMENT IN THE STATE OF Maryland, we joined a Baptist church up there in Jessup. It was a small, quaint venue with very loving Christian people. We continue to stay in touch with some who went there with us. When I think of that church, I remember a number of things, but one I choose to share is the time a Southern Gospel quartet came to sing. If you know anything about their performances, you learn that they can have a great time with each other and with the audience that's listening. During one such occasion, this particular group provided the opportunity for anyone in the audience who wanted to sing a song to do so — an open microphone sort of thing. What I learned about southern gospel sings is it brings in all kind of folks — and this time was not an exception. During the second set of singing, the lead singer told the congregation there that anyone who wanted to sing a song can do so now. Well, an older woman raised her hand and went to the microphone and commenced to singing, or trying to sing the song, Take My Cup and Fill it Up. Now, I've heard a lot of singing at the church houses in my time, but this one ranks up there, or down there, with one of the worst renditions. The woman was bad off key but seemed to enjoy the limelight provided to her. Then it dawned on me, she's got to be with this gospel quartet and any minute now she's going to sing beautifully. Nope—didn't happen. After she sang all verses of the song, we all were so glad she was through that we all gave her resounding applause, which she mistakenly thought was a request for an encore performance. Wrong! Well, at that she broke into singing that song again. One of our church members named Doyle was hard of hearing and always had his hearing aid turned wide open so he could hear goings on in the church. It had gotten so bad for Brother Doyle that he commenced to turning his hearing aid all the way down and in direct response to the old woman's second stab at singing, everyone in the church could hear him loudly say, "Do something with that cup!" After the performance, I spoke with the lead singer of the quartet and told him I thought the woman was with them, and he told me he allowed to her sing the second time because he thought she was a church member of ours. Neither was true.

Just Got Married

BACK IN 1976, FAYE AND I MARRIED AND WENT TO DISNEY World for our honeymoon. No, we didn't stay in one of those fancy resorts, or the Holiday Inn, or even a Mom and Pop place. We stayed in her uncle's camper hull that was perched on top of the truck bed. We stopped the first night after marrying at the Rocket Hotel in Cordele and lit out for Orlando. When we left the church in Hawkinsville, the gas gauge on Uncle Homer Dean's truck read three-quarters full. We were getting excellent gas mileage because all the way down to Ocala it still read three-quarters of a tank of gas — until. After getting off the interstate we took the state roads all the way into Orlando and the KOA Campground where we had reservations. Just a few miles onto the state highway system, Uncle Homer Dean's truck began to sputter and eventually stopped in the road. Well, I just knew it wasn't out of gas because it still read three-quarters full. Fortunately for us, we were within sight of a farmer's home where I asked to use the phone to call Faye's uncle about his truck stopping in the road. He laughed when I told him what happened and he then told me that the gas gauge had not worked for a long, long time. After hanging up the phone, I asked the farmer for some assistance in getting the truck some gas. I told him the following: "We just got married and have run out of gas." He replied, "I bet y'all have!" I didn't understand his response then, but understand it now. So, since the farmer had his own gas pump back behind his home, he placed it in a gas can and I placed its contents in the truck. The rest of our honeymoon we kept a closer watch on that truck's gas gauge.

A Dime from Bigmama

I COME FROM A HUGE FAMILY. ON MY DADDY'S SIDE, I HAD 45 cousins. On my mama's side, I had 26 cousins. Every week during my formative years in the 1960s, my daddy's older brother, my Uncle J.B., would pick up me and my sister Susan in our town of Adel and take us to my daddy's mama's home in Nashville, Georgia, 12 miles away. That occurred every Friday night. We affectionately called Daddy's mama Bigmama. It wasn't because she was big in stature but rather in strength. She was only 5 feet tall and weighed less than a hundred pounds soaking wet. As I recall, every Saturday morning she would make me feel very special by taking me into her bedroom and giving me a dime. Yes, a dime. And she would tell me that because I was very special to her and that she really couldn't afford to give every one of her grandchildren a dime, that that dime was mine. It made me extremely grateful and special—until. Decades later, my wife and I were the honchos for family reunions on my daddy's side of family and while talking about Bigmama to the large gathering, I mentioned the aforementioned story. It brought a lot of laughter from those present that day. You see, that day I learned that Bigmama had given a dime to each of my cousins when they came to visit, and had told them the same story about how special each was to her. Bigmama, you remain very special to me.

Running up on Johnny

DECADES AFTER OUR INFAMOUS TRIP TO SAINT AUGUSTINE Beach, I ran up on none other than my old friend Johnny. My wife and I traveled down to Valdosta to attend one of my cousin's husband's funeral and stopped at the local pizza joint to catch a quick lunch. We had originally planned to eat at the fried chicken joint, but it was so busy we chose to go next door. As fate would have it, a couple came in with their grandson soon after we were seated and I told Faye that I thought the man was my old friend Johnny. I waited until I heard the woman with him address him as John. I was right. So, I went up to him and asked him if his name was Johnny Day and he said yes. I told him I was a blast from the past and asked him if he remembered me.

He replied, Bobbie Joe Singletary! A little upset but not showing it, I told him my actual name, and of course, he remembered me. We were a part of the original Bay Street Bums, all living on West Bay Street in Adel. I really don't know why they called it Bay Street because it was not on a bay but it was on a street. We reminisced for a while, exchanged telephone numbers and a couple of weeks later I telephoned him and invited him and his wife Debbie to visit us anytime. All because the fried chicken joint was full.

Running up on my other friend Johnny

WHEN MY SON PLAYED HIGH SCHOOL FOOTBALL, I TAUGHT him to never underestimate the other guy, no matter what he looks like. Case in point, I shared with him the following true story. The only year I played high school football was in the ninth grade. I was only 130 pounds soaking wet, but I tried out for the team. I learned very quickly what one of our coaches thought of my football future. We had one guy on the team named Johnny and he had only one arm. I kind of felt sorry for him since we were responsible for showing the coaches our prowess in blocking and tackling and such. After we got through with our warm up drills, Coach Hobbs proceeded to pair us off. In the back of my mind I was still feeling sorry for Johnny and just knew he was in for it. In the coach's infinite wisdom, he paired me and Johnny up. A part of me didn't want to but I did want to make the team so we proceeded through the drills. And Johnny gave me all I could handle and more. I learned a very valuable lesson that day—never, ever, underestimate the other guy. As fate would have it, decades later my son and I were attending the local

Fall fair held in Perry, Georgia, and ran into the one and only Johnny, still with only one arm. I introduced my son to Johnny and shared this story with him. I never tried out for the football team again.

Sitting on the Floor

IN THE LATE 1980S, I FINALLY GOT STATIONED AT THE closest AF base to my home town, Moody AFB outside of Valdosta. At the time, it was a Tactical Air Force base with F-16 fighter jets there. I inherited a very nice office building and personal office area that my predecessor and his team personally renovated. The office also came with the finest furnishings I had ever had in my then 17 year AF career. Those things not made of the finest wood in my newly inherited office were of the finest in leather. It all looked great.

Prior to my predecessor's leaving, he took me to the offices of those he had worked alongside with from other military professions. After he left, one of those professionals gave me a phone call requesting that he be able to keep his base post office box he had had for the past three years. My postal officer had told me that we were running short of those lock boxes designed for those residing in the dormitories and for assigned JAG and medical doctors. The officer who asked to keep his lock box did not reside in a dormitory on base nor was he a JAG or medical doctor, so I declined his request. That occurred late one workday afternoon.

The next morning when I arrived at my office all my furnishings were gone—all of it, except my phone. Unbeknownst to me, my predecessor had worked a deal with the officer in question that if he could have and maintain a post office lock box, he could keep the fine office furnishings that he furnished. So, until we could find some other office furnishings later that day, I literally sat on the floor in that AF office. Oh, during the remainder of my watch, the officer in question did not have his own base post office lock box.

First UGA Football Game

IN 2006, MY CHURCH FRIEND HAROLD INVITED ME TO GO along with him, his daughter, and a nephew of his to my first ever UGA football game at Sanford Stadium. It was 23 September and the Bulldogs were playing the Buffs of Colorado. It was an unseasonably warm, no, it was a hot September day in Athens. My wife suggested I wear jeans instead of a pair of shorts, and I did so. I also wore one of my UGA red t-shirts. We sat very near the stadium's jumbo-tron, where the sun continually shined on us. Harold and our entourage all wore shorts. Before halftime, I was sweating up something—dripping sweat. By the time the game was over I was sunburned, so much so that my face was matching the redness of my t-shirt. I was miserable. But I saw the Bulldogs that day in a come from behind win—14-13. GO DAWGS!

Turning the Concentrate into Wine

In 1996, I was ordained a Deacon in my Southern Baptist Church. One of my roles at the time was to ensure the elements were properly prepared for the quarterly Communion service. A fellow Deacon named Mike, also newly appointed, and I, were responsible for acquiring the grape juice that morning. So, I went to the local supermarket and picked up the frozen concentrate kind of juice that our senior Deacons suggested. However, once we began to mix up the frozen concoction, we learned we had the white grape juice. We immediately searched for some red food coloring, but there was none. So, I had to make another trip to the supermarket, this time picking up the appropriate red grape juice. Some substitutions may work in some churches, but white grape juice use for Communion Services in Southern Baptist Churches will never, ever do.

Bossman and the Load of Wood

MY TERM OF ENDEARMENT FOR MY FATHER-IN-LAW WAS Bossman. He was the boss man. My pa-in-law never did anything half-way, he did everything full bore. That included hauling loads of firewood on the back of his pickup truck, over flowing loads, I might add. One day he was driving through nearby Cochran, Georgia with one of those loads and his grandson Scotty Wayne saw him. According to Scotty Wayne, here's the rest of the story: Scotty gave his Papa enough time, 11 miles, to drive home to Hawkinsville with that load of wood. Scotty said he called his grandparent's home phone and in a muffled voice pretended to be someone else asking Mema if he could talk to Mr. Brown. Mema put Papa on the phone and Scotty Wayne asked him if he had just got home from Cochran, and he said yes. Scotty then asked him if he was hauling a huge load of firewood on his old blue pickup truck, and he said yes — what about it! Scotty then told him that a piece of his firewood fell from his pickup truck and struck the grill of his vehicle, damaging the front end — to the tune of $250 worth of damage. Bossman went ballistic. Now that's not a Southern term but it's better to use it here rather than to tell you what Bossman's actual response was to Scotty's phone call. Mema told us later that Papa was so bothered by the phone call that the hung up the phone, only for Scotty, in disguised voice, to redial. Before Scotty Wayne could explain to his Papa that the phone call was a hoax, he lit right in to him. Finally, Scotty Wayne told his Papa that it was him. Papa told him I'll get you back. To my knowledge, Papa never did.

Bossman and Uncle Pete

Even though Bossman never got back at Scotty Wayne, the story goes that he did for his brother-in-law, Pete. Decades ago, Uncle Pete asked Bossman to ride and steer behind him while Uncle Pete pulled a car from the Macon area on a 40 mile trek back to Hawkinsville. Bossman agreed. However, on that trip, apparently Uncle Pete never braked, and on two occasions the car Bossman was steering passed alongside Uncle Pete's car. By the time they pulled into Hawkinsville, Bossman was white knuckled and swore to Uncle Pete that he would eventually return the favor. Bossman said it took him 25 years to do so. He asked Uncle Pete to ride and steer behind him this time. And Uncle Pete agreed, forgetting what happened 25 years before. Bossman said that when he looked in his rearview mirror, Uncle Pete was attempting to light a cigarette. He said that when they arrived in Hawkinsville, Uncle Pete still had the unlit cigarette in his mouth. Pay back.

A Wish from Santa

SEVERAL CHRISTMASES AGO MY WIFE AND I WENT UP TO Blue Ridge, Georgia to ride on the Santa Claus train. The train ride involved a ten-mile trip back and forth up a rail line there with Santa, Mrs. Claus, and a bunch of Elves prancing around bringing good cheer. That same year, similar to decades of no national college football championships, the Bulldogs of UGA fell short of another opportunity - again. Seizing my opportunity to do what I could for that cause, I asked Santa on that train ride the following request: Santa, please before I die please grant me this wish, one more college national championship for the mighty Bulldog Nation. After pondering Santa replied, "It depends on how much time you got left, little boy!" He was not the real Santa Claus!

Billy Lee

My daddy was a member of the Greatest Generation. You know the ones who endured the Great Depression of the 1930s as children and then went off to war during the 1940s as young adults. He went in to the U.S. Navy at the ripe old age of 17 in 1942 and 21 years later retired from military service. Years later, I asked my daddy the story of how I got my name. This is what he told me. When I was born in the Summer of 1951, Daddy said most of the sailors on the ships where he served named their sons Junior. He told my mama that no son of his was going to be called Junior — or so he thought. After my birth at the Jacksonville Naval Air Station in Florida, mama and daddy were deciding what to name me since Junior was not an option for Daddy. Well, my mama in her infinite wisdom told daddy to name me after her brother Billy Lee. To which Daddy replied, "Junior is fine." I was never addressed by any of my family as Junior, just Donny.

That Boat Looks Like Mine

IN THE EARLY 1970S, I WAS ASKED BY A FORMER FAMILY member to help pull a fishing boat from South Georgia to the Salt Flats of the Gulf of Mexico. So I did. The family member pulled another boat and we set out for some fishing. However, he left it up to me to hitch the boat to my vehicle, something I had never done. As fate would have it, I failed to secure it to the hitch and while driving through Tallahassee I noticed something pass me to my right that looked strangely familiar—it looked a lot like the boat I was pulling. Fortunately, it hit nothing but a nearby ditch, where we had to retrieve it. The family member then hitched the boat properly.

Back Slapping at the Church

During our children's formative years, they all had a drug problem. Yes, we "drug" them to church every Sunday. While attending a Sunday morning service in our church in Valdosta, Georgia, my son, then around eight or nine years old, was fidgeting during the sermon. The first time he did it, I politely asked him to quit. The second time I could tell it was an annoyance to those around us. And the third time it happened, I took his arm and led him to the front porch of that church and wore his tail out. We had been sitting about four pews from the front so most of the church noticed when I was taking him out. And I didn't know that the folks in the church could hear what was happening on the front porch of the church that morning. But, afterwards I got more back slaps and compliments from the elders. My son still remembers it.

No Trees to Hide Behind

DURING AUGUST OF 1990, I WAS CALLED UP TO SERVE IN the desert during what would later be known as Operation Desert Shield and Operation Desert Storm. Prior to pulling out for the deployment, my daddy's side of the family had a fish fry for me in Nashville, Georgia. My daddy's brother, my Uncle Frank, who had also served in the U.S. Army during the late 1950s and early 1960s, fried the fish that Saturday night. One of my cousins, Ricky, was there and he was three sheets in the wind, if you know what I mean. He was a Vietnam veteran, having served as an Infantryman. Looking back on it he was probably trying to make me feel better about going over there but he told me this, "Donny, I'll be thinking of you, but at least in Vietnam I had some trees to hide behind."

A Good Phone Line

REGARDING MY DESERT SHIELD EXPERIENCE, AFTER BEING called up, thirteen of us boarded a bus from Moody AFB in South Georgia for Eglin AFB, Fort Walton Beach, Florida, and waited for military transportation to the desert. We waited for a full week. My colonel who was on the team made the call for us to head back home since all the military transport planes were only taking equipment at the time and no Airmen. After returning home, I phoned my Uncle Frank to tell him what happened. Initially he told me that we had a good phone line because he could hear me clear as a bell. It was then that I told him what had happened; and he and my family were relieved. However, for the remaining two years I kept my duffel bag and luggage in the corner of my office, just in case I was called to go again.

As fate would have it, six weeks prior to leaving on my next military assignment to Maryland, my name was chosen again. This time my colonel made a phone call to his higher ups and told them I was locked in to another military assignment that would prohibit me from finally going to the desert. It worked. However, until my Uncle Frank passed away years later, every time he would see me he would jokingly tell me, "Son, you were so sorry they wouldn't even send you to war!" He was the family jokester.

How You Feelin'?

My cousin, Ricky, was a hoot. By profession he was a Deputy Sheriff for the Lake County, Florida police force. Personally, he was funny! Case in point, when my brother Scott got married the first time, Ricky stowed away in the back seat of the newlywed's car only to pop his head up 30 minutes down the road telling them, "Surprise!" Several years later, my Daddy's brother Joe passed away and Ricky agreed to drive my Daddy and my brother Bruce all the way to Shreveport, Louisiana for the funeral. At the time my daddy owned a candy apple red 1960s model Chevrolet he kept in mint condition. They went in it and Ricky drove. After returning from the trip, Ricky raved about how much he loved that car, to which my stepmother told him that when she died he could have it. My cousin, not being outdone, on a weekly basis thereafter would telephone my stepmother and ask the following: "How you feelin' Aunt Connie?" Ricky died of a heart attack on his front porch not long afterwards.

Salty Water

DURING MILITARY BOOT CAMP, I WAS SELECTED BY OUR Training Instructor (TI) to be our flight's Dorm Chief. All that meant was that I had the responsibility for ensuring everyone was present or accounted for every time we left or showed up from place to place. Apparently the 40 members of my flight had a dislike for me, but I never knew until one fateful day I will now recount for you.

Back in the early 1970s it was believed that a steady salt intake was good for those experiencing a great deal of weather that involved heat. My boot camp occurred during August to October in South Texas, San Antonio, to be exact. And it got hot there. Every day we were issued salt tablets to place in to our canteens which were strapped on to a belt we always kept around our waists. As the Dorm Chief, I was placed strategically at the very front of each military formation we were in. That day while waiting to participate in our several daily bouts of heavy perspiration, unbeknownst to me, an Airman behind me screwed the top off my canteen and every Airmen in the flight sent their salt tablets into my one canteen. I didn't know it until I went to take a huge gulp; and spewed it out immediately. I learned a valuable lesson that day, it's tough at the top.

Clipper Queen

In military boot camp, most teams have at least one time to work in the military chow hall. Today they call them dining facilities. They'll always be chow halls to me. We had the duty twice. The first time, the Mess Sergeant asked us who had the longest arms in our bunch and he selected me. He told me all I had to do in using my long arms was to take each tray with the plates and dump the contents into one of two holes which had huge trash cans underneath. Easy enough, or so I thought. Halfway through that breakfast, the Mess Sergeant made another appearance and asked to look at our processes. Apparently the chow hall had run out of the eating utensils, commonly referred to as silverware. Unbeknownst to me, I had raked all the silverware into the trashcans which now had been taken out to the huge trash bins outside. The Mess Sergeant selected two of my flight mates to go fetch that silverware — and they did. The second time we had Chow Hall duty that same Mess Sergeant placed me in charge of cleaning all the pots and pans.

Captain, I Can't Feel My Legs

WHILE ASSIGNED IN THE AIR FORCE TO THE REPUBLIC OF South Korea in the late 1980s, I was responsible for quite a bit. One of those self-imposed responsibilities involved the assurance that all my troops stayed out of trouble, to include their own personal safety. Over there at the time they had large concrete ditches, commonly referred to as Benjo Ditches. Some of them were 8-10 feet in depth and there were no guard rails. My role was to keep my troops out of those ditches after a night on the town. The military custom in Korea was that the troops would collectively go out on the town when a new troop came in, when one was leaving, and sometimes, when neither of the two was happening. The drink of choice by the troops was a concoction called Soju, or fermented potato. The clubs served the drink in what we called an ammo bowl—frankly it was a bedpan with 10 to 20 straws in it. After a night of libation, all the troops would walk back to the AF base in what was usually a half mile trek. Often it seemed like a thousand miles. I was always the designated walker. It's similar to the designated driver rule, but we were all walking. And, after drinking several ammo bowls, most of the troops would say to me, "Captain, I can't feel my legs!" To which I always replied, "They're still there, just keep moving between the roadway and the Benjo Ditch." Fortunately, they all got to their dormitories safely.

Blood, Sweat, and Tears

IN LATE 1982, I FINALLY GOT TO BE A STUDENT AT THE AIR Force's Officer Training School located near San Antonio, Texas. I had already served as an enlisted man for over 11 years and had risen to the rank of Technical Sergeant (E-6)—so I knew something about how the AF really was. So I thought. It is there that I learned the way things really are, and the academic way things are.

The twelve-week school was the most intense I have ever endured. It was experiential learning at its best. The first six weeks we were lower classman, doing what we were told to do, and the second six weeks we were upper classman, responsible for "running" the place. As best as I can recollect, there were nine squadrons under one wing. I was a member of a cadre of 100 or so in one of those specific squadrons.

In addition to keeping up with our required academics, we had to keep our dormitory room spotless at all times, to include our uniforms hanging in the closest. We also marched or ran everywhere we went—the chow hall, to the academic buildings, to the dispensary, to the Base Exchange, to the parade field, and to our own dormitory where we lodged. On every Saturday morning, we had inspections where we had to stand outside our door while an upper classman barked orders to us asking a number of questions while looking up and down our uniform for discrepancies. Speaking of discrepancies, I probably hold the record for the most. And, if you got too many you were bed posted, or were not allowed to leave the dormitory where your bed was. That happened a lot initially, but I found a way to make up for those discrepancies by earning merit points. That's where blood, sweat and tears come in.

First the blood part of this story. Numerous times during my twelve weeks there the Red Cross would come in for blood drives — and I went and received three merit points. I would have given my blood more often but they told me there was a grace period in between giving. Second the sweat part. The Officer Training School had a chapel which offered the Officer Trainees the opportunity to serve on their Sunday morning choir. So I did, and I sweated but earned three merit points a week for that one. And now the tears part of this story. The first few nights there are Officer Training School I shed a few tears because I deeply missed my wife and two young children, ages three and one. I didn't receive any merits for that one but I was released from my bed post.

Throw an Iron to It

ONE OF MY ROLES IN THE MILITARY DURING TWO ASSIGN-
ments was that of the Postal Officer for each AF base. That
involved many facets, to include supervision of the troops
responsible for moving intra-base communications from
one office to another. Remember, this was during a time way
before email communications. I had an affection for those
mailroom troops because my first job in the AF was being
one of them. I knew they were our "ambassadors" from the
mailroom and tried to instill in them that they were to be
professional at all times, to include immaculate military
dress. A brand new troop was assigned to the mailroom and
for the life of me I cannot remember his name. Usually I never forget a name or a face. Nonetheless, one day soon after
the new troop came on board, my Postal Non-commissioned
Officer (NCO) gave me a phone call and said that the Wing
Commander's office had just called them complaining about
the new troop's military uniform and that he looked like he
had slept in it. I told the NCO to order the young troop to
go change his uniform into a sharper one, and he did. How-

ever, the young troops told his boss that all his uniforms were dirty and the one he was wearing was the only clean one he had. I told the NCO to tell the young troop to go back to his dorm room and throw an iron to his uniform before delivering any more mail that day. He did. However, after an hour passed the NCO went directly to the young troop's dorm room and found the young man literally throwing an iron to his uniform—while wearing it. The NCO had to tell him to take his uniform off to iron it. Needless to say, we kept that young man in our mailroom building, so few people would see him. Some of this stuff you just can't make up.

Favoring My Mama

My mama's people come from Northwest Georgia near the Alabama line. Growing up in South Georgia, I never got to visit and meet any of my mama's people. But I did see my daddy's people nearly every weekend. I never gave it much thought on who I looked like or who I "favored", I just knew that my daddy was my daddy and my mama was my mama. From 2001 to 2010, my wife and I agreed to honcho our daddy's family reunion each Memorial Day Weekend Sunday down near Alapaha. It was at the Mount Paron Primitive Baptist Church, where many of my daddy's ancestors are buried. My daughter-in-law who married in to our family in 2006 began attending those reunions and soon thereafter asked me why I didn't look like any of them. I couldn't answer her because I never thought about it. Several years later, my sisters and my wife and I were invited to attend a reunion on my mama's side of the family held up in the Tallapoosa, Georgia area. It is there that the mystery was unveiled. I favor my mama and her side of the family.

Sunday School in San Antonio

Back in 1982 during a military assignment to an AF base near San Antonio, Texas, our Adult Sunday School class was asked by the teacher to introduce ourselves since we had visitors. At the time Faye and I had been married for nearly six years and had two children. When it came to me I told them my name was Don Jenrette and then it was my wife's time to introduce herself. She replied, Faye Brown. Bear in mind this was a time when the majority of women in the USA didn't keep their maiden names but took their husband's. After Faye made her reply I had to make a double take. The entire room roared with laughter — not so much at Faye but for the look on my face.

Look a Little Higher

IN 1993, MY WIFE GOT HER HAIR DYED BY A GOOD GIRL-friend of hers. And I failed to notice. Here's how it happened. It was a Sunday night and not quite dark outside. Even though I had been with my wife and two children all that day, I never noticed the change in the color of my wife's hair. But apparently our children had noticed the change, and had noticed that I failed to notice. So, on the way to church our children politely asked me from the backseat of our family automobile if I noticed something different about their mama. At that I glanced over at their mama and said the following: "Oh, a new bra." To which my wife replied, "Look a little higher, Don!"

When Did They Move it to Town?

BACK IN 1982, MY WIFE'S SISTER AND HER FAMILY, ALL FIVE of them, drove from Georgia to our home in San Antonio for a vacation trip. My brother-in-law C.W. is a huge Western fan and had always wanted to see the world-famous Alamo. Well, I took him. Once we found parking in the middle of the city of San Antonio we had to walk a few blocks to finally see it. Once he laid his eyes on it in all honesty C.W. asked me: "When did they move the Alamo to town?" He was sorely disappointed that it wasn't the same one that John Wayne fought in from 1960.

No Cowboy Hat or Boots

BACK DURING THE BUILDING BOOM OF THE EARLY 1980S IN the Houston, Texas area, one of my cousins went to live and work there. We lived just down the road in San Antonio. Once I received notification I was selected for AF Officer Training School attendance, my family and I lit out for a weekend in Houston to celebrate. Once we got settled in our fancy multi-story hotel in downtown, I called my cousin on the phone and asked him and his girlfriend to come visit us there. They did so. We talked about old times and they invited us to go boot scooting with them to one of the local watering holes. First, Faye and I have been tea-totalers for years, and it was not any different then. But my cousin insisted until he asked us and found out that we didn't own a cowboy hat nor a pair of cowboy boots. Shortly he and his girlfriend left to do some boot scooting. I guess they didn't want to have folks with them at a boot scooting place that were not properly dressed. We could leave Houston but they were stuck there.

Ted Kennedy Look Alike

I'VE HEARD THAT SOMEWHERE IN THE WORLD EVERYBODY has a twin—someone who looks just like them. We found Ted Kennedy's. My wife and I were on vacation near the Grand Ole Opry House outside Nashville, Tennessee. The resort where we stayed was nice and it included musical entertainment and complimentary dinner meals. It is there we first saw and talked with the Ted Kennedy look alike. At that time, Teddy Kennedy was still alive. The look alike and his wife told us they were vacationing from their home in Boston, Massachusetts. I told him he looked a lot like Teddy Kennedy to which he replied that he got a lot of comments like that. He told me he was a Navy veteran and after we shared some war stories he loosened up some more and told me that looking like one of the Kennedys had served him well. He told me that quite frequently he is mistaken for Teddy up in Massachusetts and given perks in hotels, restaurants, taxi cab rides, Irish Parades, etc. He said he's never told them any different.

Christmas in Hawkinsville

OUR CHILDREN ARE AIR FORCE CHILDREN, OR COMMONLY referred to as Air Force brats. Ours never were brats though. From 1980 through 1994, we made the trek a few days before Christmas time from wherever we were living to a small Middle Georgia town called Hawkinsville. That's where Mema and Papa Brown lived—their maternal grandparents. The trek was never by airplane or by bus, every time by automobile. The first car was a Datsun B210 hatchback model—extremely small and cramped. Those trips were back and forth from Montgomery, Alabama, and then later from San Antonio, Texas.

Then we purchased a brand new Pontiac Bonneville from the showroom floor outside Biloxi, Mississippi, and made Christmas trips from there, and later from Rantoul, Illinois, from Valdosta, Georgia, and from Fort Meade, Maryland. One theme that remained true for all those trips was the use of a huge car top carrier. You know, the ones designed to carry extra luggage. Except, for us it carried our children's Christmas gifts, all without them ever realizing we were doing it. It was many years later that our children asked us how Santa always knew where to bring their presents. We told them. On every Christmas morning, we had each of their gifts laid out for them, all previously packed and unpacked with love and unknown to our children. Faye's father passed in 2010 and her mother passed in 2014. Oh, how we long for those Christmases with Mema and Papa Brown, and that car top carrier.

Boiled Peanuts and Claxton Fruitcake

GEORGIA COUNTRY CAVIAR IS BETTER KNOWN AS BOILED peanuts down here. Yep, and it's always good with something cold, iced cold. Another Georgia made food specialty is the world famous Claxton Fruitcake. It's a sweet flavored delicacy commonly eaten at Christmas time and at the end of each calendar year. While stationed in the Air Force at a base in South Korea in the late 1980s, I refereed basketball and football games at the base. During one of those games I noticed one of the players wearing my beloved black and red colors of the University of Georgia Bulldogs. We struck up a conversation and I learned he was the Officer in Charge of the base's Air Terminal. Along with his job came the responsibility of ensuring Airmen were properly provided the opportunity for an airplane seat back to the world. That's what we called back to the States. Oh, also since the commercial airliner was on contract with the Department of Defense, the ride was compliments of Uncle Sam.

Here's how the procedure to board the plane was supposed to work: in order for an Airman to receive an airplane seat back to the world, he or she had to be on official leave status. Since only one airplane came in and out of the base once a week, on Thursdays, you prayed that there would be enough room for you. It never happened that way because most everyone wanted to go back to the world during Christmas time. Some Airmen had to use several days of their accrued leave time simply waiting for their name to make it to the top of the passenger manifest. Since my new friend and I were both Air Force captains and UGA football fans extraordinaire, we struck up a friendship. As it got closer to Christmas, I asked my new friend if there was a way I could get my name placed up toward the top of the passenger manifest. He told me if I could get him some boiled peanuts and a Claxton Fruitcake, along with my official leave paperwork, I could board the last plane before Christmas. So, I snail mailed my wife and asked her to send both—pronto. However, at the time she and our children were living in Illinois, so she asked her mama to mail it to me pronto. And she mailed it, I got it, and so did my friend. I made it to my family for Christmas. How's the old saying go: "It's not what you know, but who you know."

Almond Joy Leis

I WORKED FOR THE DEPARTMENT OF DEFENSE FOR 43 years and have many fond memories. One of the last ones I'll share with you now. Periodically my team of six associates and I would put on a training session which consisted of five full days of training and education in all things related to random drug testing and substance abuse prevention education protocols. Over the years, we had dozens of these but something happened during the last training sessions in which I was a part. When I discussed the area of addictions and the nature and science of it I included information on my favorite candy bar of all time—the Almond Joy. Now this is not a commercial for them, it's just my favorite of all time. My spiel went something like this; if someone begins to hide their alcohol or drugs or pornographic materials, or anything they cannot seem to live without, that person just might have an addiction. That's when I would share about my Almond Joy "addiction" but that I had not gotten to the point of hiding them from my loved ones or from others. Well, unknown to me on the last day of my last training session, the class leader from Hawaii came up to me and placed a leis around my neck as a gesture of respect and hospitality. And on the leis, several of them I might add, were the snack sized Almond Joys. I was elated and deeply appreciative for that gesture. Oh, it took me months to finally finish eating all those Almond Joys.

Fiat 500

Several years ago, during a business trip to the Washington D.C. area, I flew into the Baltimore-Washington International Airport, also known as BWI. Once on the ground there, I went to the car rental counter to receive the keys to the transportation I would use to get around to the locations I had planned to visit. Well, I must have picked a wrong time because the only thing they had left was a Fiat 500. I don't know if you're familiar with those, but they make the VW Beetle look and feel like a Lincoln Continental. The rental car attendant, after eyeballing me, suggested I wait for the next rental car that was being turned in. Please bear in mind that while eyeballing me he saw my 280-pound body on a six-foot frame. Way too big for the Fiat 500. But sensing I was running behind and needing to get to my first stop on the trip, I reluctantly accepted that car - wrong move.

First, once I did manage to get in that thing, the top of my head rubbed against the top of the inside roof. Second, because of my long legs, I tried to adjust the seat so I could stretch out a little more, but that did not work either. And third, if I thought pouring into that car was difficult, that was easy-peasy compared to when I had to pile out of it—time and again during that trip. I learned a valuable lesson: wait for the next rental car, it's got to be more form fitting than a Fiat 500.

Listening to Lewis Grizzard

To you who may not be familiar with the late, great Lewis Grizzard, Google his name and YouTube some of his humorous performances and read his many books. Lewis was a native Georgian, a UGA graduate from the 1960s, and a funny Southerner. During 1988 and 1989, I was stationed in the Air Force over in the Republic of South Korea, many, many miles away from my native Georgia. Fortunately, while there without my family I met and befriended four other native Georgians. They called us the Georgia Mafia. When we talked our Southernese, no one else could understand what we were putting out. My four AF friends were from Lake Hartwell, Folkston, Macon, and Winder, and of course me, from Adel.

Most weekends we were fortunate enough to have some time away from our long days at work. And when I packed my belongings for my year away from my family, I packed my cassette tapes of none other than Lewis Grizzard. On Friday and Saturday nights we collectively would gather at my apartment on the AF base and one of my friends would bring his cassette player and we would listen and get home sick and experience huge belly laughter, just from listening to Lewis. Later on, some of our Yankee friends were asking us what all the laughter was about coming from my apartment so we invited them in one time. All I can say is, it must be a Southern thing, without exception none of them laughed at Lewis' story. We wound up having to explain what he was saying and the context from which they flowed. Still no laughter. That was the first, last, and only time we invited Yankees into our fold to hear some Lewis Grizzard. He left us much too early, in 1994, and is sorely missed.

Bob's Conga

HERE'S ANOTHER KOREA STORY. THE FIRST FEW MONTHS there at the AF base I lodged in an old tin building located on a hill and had to share a common bathroom area with a hootch mate. His name was Bob and his job was serving as our Finance Officer. One thing you learn early in the military is not to mess with the cops nor anyone associated with your pay records. I was in like Flynn with Bob. On Friday nights, every single Friday night, after we got back to our hooch, Bob would crank up the sound on his record player, place an LP on it, yes, the vinyl kind, and play his favorite tune — Conga, from none other than Gloria Estefan and the Miami Sound Machine. You could set your clock by it. It wasn't long thereafter that I was hand-picked by our new Base Commander to be his Executive Officer and I had to change residences, much nicer, with my own private bath. No more Conga. However, when I hear that song today it takes me back to late Friday afternoons in a faraway land when I and a fellow AF officer listened to his record player.

Snail Mail in Guam

CARE PACKAGES ARE SPECIAL TO THOSE SERVING IN THE U.S. military overseas. It means someone back in the world still thinks of you and sends a mail package of various and sundry things that remind you of home. It happened a lot for me and my wife, Faye. One such time was while we were on the tiny island of Guam. When I got my orders in 1978 that we were going to spend the next two years over there, I looked it up in the Encyclopedia Brittanica at the Library under the book labeled G. I thought it was in the Caribbean, but quickly learned it was not.

Guam is a U.S. territory located 1500 miles from the Philippine Islands. It is 32 miles long and 12 miles wide, and at the time was the home for 100,000 people, Guamanians and U.S. military. As was the custom, Faye's mother would periodically mail us care packages, even with taped messages from her and the family so we could listen to them on what was happening back home in Georgia.

One such care package arrived that caused a great deal of concern for the postal workers there. They even called in the

K9 drug sniffing dogs and the AF Office of Special Investigation professionals. All because of a "suspicious" package addressed to us from Georgia. I was personally called in to the post office to open the package in their presence. First of all, the outward appearance of the care package was stained and caused the drug dog to alert on it. I began to sweat bullets. At the time my job there was one of a cadre of drug and alcohol addiction counselors responsible for counseling those with addictions. And here I was before cops and postal folks with that care package to be opened.

Upon opening the package, it reeked of a rotten smell, which we learned upon further inspection was over ripened tomatoes that poured out over the entire contents, eventually pouring out to the outer wrapping. After they had found no contraband, they chuckled and handed over the contents of the care package and told me to have a good day. Faye and I were picking tomato seeds off everything in the package for days. We asked her folks not to mail any produce to us anymore while overseas.

We Can't Keep Them Magazines

During one of my Stateside AF assignments, one of my tasks was that of the Postal Officer. My third boss in line to the top was a full Colonel in charge of the entire Wing of 5000+ military and civilian Airmen. On the first duty day after the New Year, that full Colonel gave me a personal telephone call early in the morning asking me where his sports magazine was that was addressed to his office. I explained to him that since we were at the mercy of the downtown United States Postal Service office, as soon as it came in my postal team would ensure he received his copy.

Apparently he was not satisfied with that answer. He told me that my postal team probably had his copy of the magazine and was already reading it before he saw it. Thinking initially that he was joking, I realized he was deadly serious and assured him we would get a copy of the magazine to him that day. He said he wanted it before lunch. So, being a good little Captain, I personally went to the Base Exchange and purchased a magazine he was demanding off the rack and hand delivered it to my Colonel's executive officer, a fellow Captain.

Weeks later, I was waiting at my local barber shop and saw that full Colonel receiving his weekly haircut while I waited for mine. While waiting for my hair cut, I began thumbing through the many magazines that the barber had in his waiting area but could not find a specific one that was usually there. After the Colonel left, I hopped in the chair for my own haircut and asked our barber where the specific magazine was that I could not find. He told me, "We can't keep them magazines." I then learned that the full Colonel always took a copy of that specific magazine with him. Case solved.

Five Course Meal

My last military assignment was serving as the Deputy Inspector General for a joint military organization. That job required more travel for me than the previous 21 years of military service combined. During one of my business trips to Europe, my military officer counterpart and I had three legs to accomplish, first to Naples, Italy, then on to Incirlik, Turkey, and finally to Ramstein, Germany. On the flight from Italy to Turkey we wound up on one of the European flights in first class all by ourselves. I still don't know how that happened, but we took it and at the American taxpayer costs of a coach ticket. After our airplane began to level off we each had our own airline attendant to serve us drinks and a meal. After having my soft drink, my flight attendant handed me a sheet of paper with what I thought were the choices of the inflight meal. I made my choice and choked it down quickly since the flight was a relatively short one. But, unbeknownst to me, it was only the first course in a five-course meal! Trying not to be embarrassed, I quickly scarfed down each one of the courses in record speed. Thinking back on it, I don't think I even took the time to taste. My military officer counterpart told me later he noticed I was eating at record speed and had chosen not to eat everything brought to him. All I could think of every time the food was present- ed to me was my Ma Smith's insistence that we always clean our plates. Old habits are hard to break.

The Curt Rambus Look

GROWING UP, MY SPORT WAS BASKETBALL. LOOKING BACK on it, it was cheap and had less physical contact than football. After I left for the Air Force at the age of 20 and a single man, I would spend weekends at the local base gymnasium playing that wonderful game. But I learned something. As time went on, many, many times I was the only white guy playing those games. I learned something else about people's perceptions. Initially when I stepped on the court the other players assumed since I looked like I couldn't play a good game I was treated as such. Until I showed them I "had game". As a matter of fact, long before I had Lasik eye surgery I wore eyeglasses all the time. That included wearing the Clark Kent Superman style eyeglasses on the basketball court. Yes, the same look that the Los Angeles Lakers' basketball player named Curt Rambis had. Again, you can't tell the book by looking at the cover.

Debbie Grooben

HERE'S ANOTHER PA-IN-LAW STORY. ONE DAY WHILE AS-sisting my pa-in-law in his garage he asked me to make a phone call for him. It was long before cell phone days and easy access to whomever you are trying to call. He had a black wall phone and the Hawkinsville, Georgia phone book that even I could tear in half. My pa-in-law asked me to look up Debbie Grooben and to find out a good time for Mema to pick up her dog there. Well, that seemed easy enough. So I looked under the Gs for Grooben and there was none. Not being outdone I then looked under the Js, not there. Then I looked under the Hs in case Debbie's last name had that silent letter. No luck. I was befuddled and finally asked my pa-in-law to see if he could find the telephone number. With that he opened up the Hawkinsville phone book and looking under the Ds found Debbie's Grooming. He asked me if he needed to call that number or should I. I told him I could handle that and did so.

Let's Stop

One weekend my wife and I went with her parents from Hawkinsville to the nearby town of Cochran for a barbeque supper. Since their car was roomier than ours, they insisted I be the driver for that 11 minute trip, and I did so. On the way, while passing the county line liquor store, I noticed that one of my wife's cousin's husband's truck was parked beside the establishment. At that I mentioned to my in-law's and my wife that I thought that was Fred's truck back there and sure would like to see him again. Then we ate our supper in Cochran. Unbeknownst to my kinfolk in the car, when we got close to the liquor store where Fred was I slowed down to make that right-hand turn. At that my ma-in-law got very uncomfortable and said to me, "Don, what are we doing in my car pulling in to a liquor store?" To which I replied, "To say hey to Fred." She immediately told me not to stop her car there and for us to get back on the road quickly! After I got back on the main road I asked her why she didn't want to see Fred, she told me that was not the reason for not stopping to see Fred. She said this, "Somebody from the church might drive by and see our car in the liquor store parking lot!"

Aunt Vena

My wife's Uncle James served in the United States Marine Corps and after separating from that military service got married to an Italian girl from Waterbury, Connecticut in the 1950s. She went by Aunt Vena. Decades later, after Uncle James passed away, my in-laws wanted to visit his widow one more time so we took the trip together. After resting up there the first night we went to the cemetery the next day where Uncle James was buried and noticed something peculiar. When Aunt Vena buried him, she purchased double head stones with not only Uncle James' name on there but also her name. Upon gazing at the name next to Uncle James' I asked Aunt Vena, the woman I had known for nearly 20 years, whose name was listed as Verna on that tombstone. She replied, "Mine." I was flabbergasted. Then I asked her this, "So if your name is really Verna, then why do we all call you Vena?" She replied, "I don't know."

New Jersey Rest Stop

IN THE 1990S, MY PA-IN-LAW AND I TRAVELED UP TO THE Northeastern U.S. On our way back down we stopped at one of those super-duper rest stops in New Jersey. Here's what happened. Upon entering the men's restroom, the entry doors opened automatically. Then after using the urinals my pa-in-law asked me where the jiggler was so he could flush it. I told him to step back and it would automatically flush it. Then we went to the sink to wash our hands and he asked me where the faucet handle was and I told him that a sensor would allow the water to wet his hands for washing. Then we went to dry our hands and he asked where the paper towels were and I explained to him that he had to place his hands under the contraption on the wall and it would dry his hands. After all that and while walking back to the truck he made the following remark, "I'm glad that's all I had to do in there."

Blood in the Crab Legs

YEARS AGO, MY WIFE AND I TOOK A VACATION TRIP TO SPEND some precious time with an old AF buddy and his wife in Oceans Springs, Mississippi. Ocean Springs is just across the bay from Biloxi. At the time, I had never tried crab legs but my friend took us to one of the casino buffets, and all you care to eat crab legs. Well, after our waitress brought us each a huge plate of them, I tried my best to crack open what I would learn later was fittin' to eat. Well into my second plate of them things, I noticed something odd about my crab legs. I even called our waitress over and told her that my crab legs had blood in them. To which she replied, "Honey, that's your blood on them crab legs." Unbeknownst to me, I had inadvertently cut up my fingers trying my best to open those crab legs. Just a tad bit embarrassed, I asked her if she had any band aids, which she did but she said I'd have to put them on my own fingers. It worked. Since that time, I've eaten many a crab leg and have the cracking routine down to a science and an art. No more blood in my crab legs.

White Diamond Grill VW

HERE'S ANOTHER PA-IN-LAW STORY. THIS OCCURRED BEfore my time in the Brown Family. For decades, my pa-in-law and his son-in-law C.W. worked in a production plant environment off Guy Paine Road in Macon. As was the custom, my pa-in-law would ask for assistance to get VWs to his garage for repair. This one time it was C.W. that helped. Then and now there is a barbeque joint called the White Diamond Grill near the intersection of Georgia 247 and Old Georgia 96. My pa-in-law told C.W. to drive a VW that would be parked outside that restaurant with the keys already in it. Remember, this was a time when most people left their car keys in the ignition for no fear of losing it. Well, C.W. did just what he was asked and upon driving up to my pa-in-law's garage he noticed the VW was not the color he was looking for. C.W. had jumped in the wrong VW and drove it 20 minutes south to Hawkinsville. He would say later that he couldn't understand why its owner wanted a tune up since it was running very good. After my pa-in-law told C.W. it was the wrong VW, he shut it off. And as fate would have it, it failed to crank up again. They called the White Diamond Grill and told them what had happened so the owner would not be too surprised when he or she came out to see it was gone. They also left word to the owner that the VW would not crank but that my pa-in-law would get it running again and get it to them within the hour. He did so. From then on, when any of us assisted in driving a car for my pa-in-law, we made sure it was the right one.

Europe and Uncle Frank

DURING THE 1950S, FOUR OF MY BIG MAMA JENRETTE'S five sons were serving in the U.S. military. My daddy and his older brother, my Uncle J.B. were in the Navy; my Uncle Joe was in the Air Force, and my Uncle Frank was in the Army. My daddy told me this story. One Saturday night in Germany, my daddy went for a night on the town in one of the taverns over there. He said he and his fellow sailors arrived early and closed the place down at 2 a.m. the next morning. Daddy said that earlier in the evening he heard very familiar laughter but didn't stop his drinking to check it out any further. Apparently, it must have been a pretty good sized tavern. When the tavern's proprietor shut the place down and they all began to shuffle out that is when Daddy saw where that laughter came from earlier that evening. It was his brother, Franklin Delano Jenrette. And, since time was of the essence, they had no time to reminiscence and went their separate ways — one to the ship and one to the garrison.

In the Deer Stand

A BROTHER-IN-LAW OF MINE LOVES TO DEER HUNT. HE took all three of his boys when they were growing up and now frequently takes his three grandsons. This story is even before those times. Here's how it was told to me. He was way up in the deer stand very early one cold winter morning with two layers of clothes on and an extra hoodie. You know the one with the fabric to pull up over your head to keep the cold off you. Well, as fate would have it, he got the strong urge to do Number Two way up there in the deer stand that morning. Not being outdone and not wanting to climb all the way down the tree, he pulled down all he was wearing to relieve himself. After that he pulled up his clothes and continued to wait for the deer to come. My brother-in-law said as the morning progressed he would get a strong whiff of feces but only when he turned his head a particular way. Unfortunately for him, the weather that morning did not get warmer but colder. At that he felt the need to pull the hoodie up over his head. It was then that he learned where the stench was coming from. Hey, I don't believe if that had happened to me I would have ever told that story to anybody.

Slip Away in Mr. Hill's Juke Joint

Go back with me to 1970. I was finishing up high school that Spring and working part time for Mr. Daugherty and Railway Express Agency. That outfit is now out of business but is very similar to what we now know as UPS or Federal Express. During the weekday evenings and on Saturdays at noon time, we would go to Mr. Hill's barbeque joint which was located less than a couple of football fields away from our work. We would always get his pork barbeque sandwich with the meat falling off the bun. Well, one Saturday night prior to going to the weekend dance at the Other Place, I got a hankering for one of those pork sandwiches. As I got out of my 1964 Chevrolet Impala heading into Mr. Hill's restaurant, I did not notice all the Cadillacs with wide white wall tires, 4 and 3 hole Buicks with curb feelers and such. Upon entering the barbeque joint I quickly noticed it was overflowing with people — and I was the only white dude in the place. Unbeknownst to me, I was barging in on a private party. After taking three steps into the juke joint, I noticed four things very quickly. Number one, two men immediately blocked my entry point; number two, the juke box was playing the song Slip Away; number three, everyone in the place had eyes on me; and number four, I didn't see Mr. Hill. As the two men behind me began reaching into their pants pockets, I sped up my steps and hollered out for Mr. Hill for immediate help. Then he appeared and immediately asked me, "Boy, what you doing in here?" To which I replied, "I just wanted one of your sandwiches." Continuously moving my feet toward Mr. Hill, he whisked me away out his kitchen door and told me to run. And I ran. I never went back to Mr. Hill's juke joint on Saturday nights.

Accent at Keesler

I'M SOUTHERN THROUGH AND THROUGH. EVEN AT THE AGE of 60 something, I have never left my native tongue behind - even when I was asked to do so. Here's the story. It was the early 1980s where I was serving as a Lieutenant in the Air Force and in dual roles — one, as an Instructor and two, as a Squadron Section Commander. Both were very demanding jobs but I never realized it until much later. During one of the meetings held by my commanding officer, an AF O-6, Colonel, he was going over my performance and apparently was extremely pleased with it. However, he had one concern and stated it this way, "Lieutenant", he said, "you'll be a fine officer if you would work on your accent." Knowing what he was trying to say, I immediately replied the following, "Sir, with all due respect, I think I've got my accent down pretty well." I won't tell you his actual response but he did tell me he was through with our discussion that day. By the way, that Colonel was originally from way out west in LaGrange, Georgia, but you couldn't tell it by his accent.

Who's In Charge?

HERE'S YET ANOTHER AF STORY. THIS ONE IS ALSO WHILE I was at Keesler AFB, Mississippi. I was serving as an Executive Officer and was the highest ranking military member in my building, while my boss, an AF Captain, had gone for lunch on that specific day. As fate would have it, the Center Commander, an AF two-star general, entered our entrance to the building and an NCO immediately called the place to attention. Immediately I ran out to meet him and asked him if we could be of assistance. He then asked me, "Who's in charge here, Lieutenant?" I immediately replied the following, "Apparently, you are sir!" He told me later that I would go far in the Air Force. I was just telling the truth.

Over Taken

Back in the 1990s, my wife and I went up to the Big Apple to visit Lady Liberty. You know, the one that's stood tall over New York Harbor for over a century. As is the custom, we took the Liberty Island Ferry from Battery Park heading out to the Statue. That day was damp and rainy so the entire ferry boat was wet and slippery. Once we boarded and wanted to get a better view, we went to the top deck. And the view was beautiful—the Statue ahead of us and Manhattan behind. On our way down the wet steps, Faye and I got separated and a few moments later I heard several thumps and groaning at the end of those steps. To myself I was thinking some fool done fell down all 12-16 steps. I know that's not proper English, but that's the way I sometimes think. To my surprise, the person I called a fool was my wife and she was writhing in pain. I learned later that because of the fall she skinned her back up something fierce. While everybody was filing off that ferry, only one dear old lady stopped to see what was wrong with her asking, "Honey, are you okay?" Not wanting her to know that my wife had just slipped down the flight of stairs, I replied, "She's just overtaken by the Statue."

Limp Dish Rag

My son, Edwin, and I used to pop each other's back. How we did it was like this. Standing behind we would wrap our arms tightly around the torso and lift the other off the ground. After I was successful with the procedure on my son, it was his turn to do mine. Before the procedure, the one that gets his back popped is to loosen up and allow the process to happen. I did. But unexpectedly my son didn't have the complete grip on my torso and I immediately fell to the ground — like a limp dish rag. We still laugh about that. And, since then we've never ever tried to pop one another's backs. Neither of us likes the feeling of being a limp dish rag.

Worried What Our Children Will Look Like

BACK IN THE LATE 1960S WHEN I WAS IN MY LATER TEENS, I took the opportunity to date a few of the pretty women within a 15 mile radius of my home. I don't know where I first got the notion about taking every precaution I could to ensure I always dated pretty girls. But as time went on I grew to appreciate how my children would look — specifically if their mama was pretty. Here's a story on how that almost went awry. Early one Saturday evening while taking my obligatory bath before going to the local dance, my friend Wendell, from a town over from Adel, called me on the phone. Wendell and I worked for the same man kicking boxes during weekday evenings. The only other time I remember Wendell calling me for a night with the girls was the time we went to Tifton. Wendell's car was much, much nicer than mine. His was a 1968 Ford Torino with racing stripes down the side and mine was a 1964 Chevy Impala that when I stopped at the gas station I asked them to fill it up with oil and check the gas. I learned back then that the girls always liked the nicer cars.

On that particular night, when we arrived at a place called The Woods in downtown Tifton, we didn't have any girls with us. But that changed. Wendell had a few years on me and told me to follow his lead right while pointing out where he spotted two good looking girls. As we approached them we could tell they were annoyed by the two other boys trying to get them on the dance floor. At that, Wendell went up to one of the girls and shouted out, "Cousin Jody!" Following his lead I did the following to the other girl. To my amazement those girls gave us huge bear hugs and we danced the rest of the night away. That's that story.

Somehow remembering the great time that Wendell and I had in Tifton, I anticipated another great time from this second call. This is what he told me. "Donny, how about a double date with me tonight?" To you who are not familiar with what a double date is, it's when two guys take out two girls in the same vehicle and remain with each throughout the night. I immediately told him yes but inquired who the girls were. Wendell told me one of them was his next door neighbor that he'd tried to date for years. So, I deduced that she was not going to be my date. So, I asked him the all-important question, "What does the other girl look like?" And with no hesitation, he assured me she was a very sweet girl. I had heard that kind of response before but not where I was a major participant. Wendell went on to tell me that a goal of his had been to get a date with his next door neighbor but she wouldn't go it alone with him. So, being a good buddy, I told him to come on.

When they pulled up in his Torino, it was just getting

dark so I rushed outside to get a quick peek at my date for that evening. His date was in the front seat with Wendell and my date was in the backseat. As I was crawling into the backseat I couldn't get a good look at my date because Wendell had purposely covered his hand over the dome light in his car. He did it while faking a yawn, but I knew immediately what was going on. Then he sped off. That night we went to Mathis City Auditorium in downtown Valdosta to hear a battle of the bands. The battle of the bands dances involved four different bands, one in each corner of the dance hall, all playing your favorite music one at a time—what's referred to now as Golden Oldies. Once we parked and proceeded to get out of the car I assisted my date from the back seat and finally got a good look at her. Bless her heart. At the time, I was six-foot one-inch tall and about 150 pounds soaking wet. My date that evening didn't make it to five-foot tall and was nearly as big around as she was tall. But Wendell was right, she was a very sweet girl.

Couldn't Find the Courthouse

My boy attended a middle Georgia two-year college his first two years of college. Since it was 30 minutes from our home, he commuted each school day. One of those days, while running late for class, he got law caught. Yep, that's southernese for being pulled over by the local police for speeding. When he got home that evening, he asked me to go to court with him for moral support, so I did.

Apparently this was not the small town judge's first rodeo. By design, he had the cases before his court that involved college students as the last ones he judged. My boy got an education that day, and so did I. The first case involved a DUI. The judge gave him 100-hours community service for running over a fire hydrant. The second case involved a lady who apparently had been before that judge in the past. Upon her entry, which was an hour and a half late, the judge asked her why she was late, to which she replied, "You won't believe me, judge." The judge replied, "You're right, but try me, Sally." The lady's excuse was, "I couldn't find the courthouse this morning." The judge replied, "You're right, I don't believe you." For those who are not familiar with how a traditional southern courthouse looks, google it.

The last case before the college students stood before that judge was a lady who was caught by the police speeding. Since the lady pled not guilty, the arresting officer gave his side the story. He said that the lady was going 50 miles over the speed limit, and his speed gun reported such. The judge, at that, asked what her defense was. She then replied, "The officer was clocking the truck I was passing, and not me." Guilty as charged.

Oh, my boy wound up paying $75 to the court and had to write a lengthy letter of apology for speeding in his fair city. A valuable lesson.

About the Author

Don Jenrette grew up in Adel, Georgia, 39 miles north of the Florida state line. At 20 years of age, he joined the United States Air Force as an enlisted member. His military assignments range from Europe, to the Far East, and throughout the United States.

Dr. Jenrette retired from active duty AF service as a commissioned officer. After military retirement, he served as a counselor for the Georgia Department of Corrections before settling in working at Robins AFB in a civil service capacity for an additional 19 years. He earned a Bachelor of Science degree (magna cum laude) in 1982 in Psychology from Troy University; a Master of Science degree in 1986 in Criminology from the University of Southern Mississippi; a Doctor of Education degree in 2004 from the University of Georgia; and a Doctor of Ministry in Pastoral Leadership in 2017 from Andersonville Theological Seminary. He has been married to Linda Faye Brown from Hawkinsville, Georgia, since 1976. They have three children, Jennifer, Roxanne, and Edwin, and five grandchildren, Tre', Jacob, Madison, Sophie, and Tucker. Dr. Jenrette is an Associate Pastor at Sandy Valley Baptist Church in Warner Robins, Georgia.

CPSIA information can be obtained
at www.ICGtesting.com
Printed in the USA
LVHW11s2133241018
594745LV00001B/127/P